Liberating Sápmi

Indigenous Resistance in Europe's Far North

Gabriel Kuhn

Liberating Sápmi: Indigenous Resistance in Europe's Far North
Gabriel Kuhn
© 2020 PM Press.

We have made every effort to identify and properly credit the images used in
this book, but it is possible that errors and omissions may inadvertently remain.
Notice of such should be sent to the publisher so that the necessary corrections
may be made in any future editions.

ISBN: 978-1-62963-712-9
Library of Congress Control Number: 2019933022

Cover by John Yates / www.stealworks.com
Interior design by briandesign

10 9 8 7 6 5 4 3 2 1

PM Press
PO Box 23912
Oakland, CA 94623
www.pmpress.org

Printed in the USA.

Contents

Preface

I grew up in a village of a thousand people in the Austrian Alps. My first association with indigenous peoples was a very romanticized notion of American Indians, a common feature in the German-speaking world.[1] Once I turned sixteen, the interest turned more serious. Instead of exotifying novels, I began to read ethnological studies and became particularly interested in the political history of indigenous peoples and anticolonial resistance.

In the mid-1990s, I accepted a research assistantship at Arizona State University. It allowed me to attend lectures in an American Indian Studies program in the making. Pawnee professor James Riding In, today a director of the program, generously put up with my many questions, took me to relevant lectures, and introduced me to other American Indian scholars. Students from Arizona's Navajo and Hopi reservations shared their experiences with me. I will forever be grateful.

Before leaving the US, I made a trip to the Lakota Pine Ridge Reservation to get a firsthand impression of the place where the American Indian Movement (AIM) made its most memorable stand of the 1970s, with AIM activists occupying Wounded Knee, the site of a gruesome massacre committed by the US Army in 1890. It was a memorable trip, and my traveling companion and I owe two Pine Ridge mechanics who managed to fix the heating in our car, which had broken down in subzero temperatures.

In the late 1990s, I spent a couple of years in Australia and New Zealand to learn more about the situation of indigenous people there. I also stayed in New Caledonia for six months after becoming obsessed with the Kanak independence struggle.

In the year 2000, I traveled to Europe's far north for the first time. I was curious about the Sámi, the region's indigenous people whom I knew comparatively little about. I remember how strikingly similar their experience of colonialism seemed to that of other indigenous peoples. The foundations of their culture—access to land and water but also their traditional spirituality and forms of social organization—had been eroded by settlers from the south who, in turn, had been sponsored by the governments of the fledgling Nordic nation-states. The disregard for the Sámi's way of life, the arrogance of their new masters, and the ruthlessness with which the latter established their rule seemed all too familiar. Material traits of Sámi culture were destroyed, spiritual practices forbidden, and forced labor policies introduced. To this day, the colonial governments benefit immensely from the exploitation of Sápmi. In the 2016 mainstream television series *Midnight Sun*, one of the first to feature Sámi culture in a more nuanced manner, a Swedish helicopter pilot enlightens a French police officer who has come to the far north to help solve the murder of a French citizen, by stating: "They have taken everything from the Sámi except for reindeer herding—probably because it is such hard work."

I moved to Sweden in 2007. At the time, it had never dawned on me to work on a book about the Sámi. My interest in indigenous peoples has crept into my work here and there, but bigger projects I clearly saw as the domain of others, first and foremost indigenous authors themselves.

Yet, after a decade of living in Sweden, I began to wonder whether I might be able to make a contribution after all. I felt there was a need for an English-language book introducing the political struggle of the Sámi to a broader audience. I knew from my travels that, in various countries, indigenous activists and their allies were interested in the Sámi but found useful material hard to access. While a body of literature on the Sámi exists in English, most publications are academic, expensive, and difficult to track down. And few focus on political—rather than anthropological or cultural—questions.

The practical conditions seemed satisfying: while not being able to speak Sámi obviously puts limits on any deeper exploration of the culture, my command of Swedish and the ability to read and understand Norwegian allows me to access political documentation and follow relevant debates. It also allows me to communicate with the vast majority of the Sámi, 90 percent of whom live in Norway and Sweden, most of them using Norwegian or Swedish as their primary language. In addition, a well-established working relationship with PM Press meant that there was a committed independent publisher willing to take on the project.

What really motivated me to work on this book, however, was my frustration over the lack of interest in the Sámi among the majority populations of the Nordic countries. I remember watching a prominent Sámi artist participate in a TV program in which Sweden-based musicians travel to Memphis, Tennessee, to play music with locals. Each episode starts with the artist having a chat with the host upon arrival. In this particular episode, the host eventually said: "So, you are a Sámi. Can you tell me a little about the Sámi? I know nothing about them." It was said nonchalantly; there was no shame or embarrassment. It was as if you were asking an ice stock sport enthusiast to tell you about ice stock sport because you didn't know anything about it, and no one could reasonably expect that you did.

Without doubt, the host meant well and is not to blame, as their approach revealed a much more profound problem: the majority of people in Sweden—as well as in Finland and, albeit perhaps to a lesser degree, in Norway—simply don't care about the Sámi.[2]

While the disregard for the Sámi people in mainstream society should have probably not come as a huge surprise, what really puzzled me was that it was not much different among political activists. Despite all pitfalls and shortcomings, almost all nonindigenous activists I knew in North America, Australia, and New Zealand aimed to be good allies to indigenous peoples. In the Nordic countries, the same circles reveal a surprising level of indifference.[3] Sometimes, matters are even worse. When I raised the question with a longtime trade unionist in Sweden, he said that, historically, even the most radical of the miners in the far north had been "racist."

This historical collision between a progress-oriented and industry-based Left on the one hand, and an indigenous people eager to preserve vast wilderness areas on the other, remains unresolved, even among left-wing activists who are more informed by autonomous and anarchist principles than traditional leftist institutions such as trade unions. For them, the contentious issues are environmentalism, animal rights, and nationalism. Is it okay for the Sámi to object to wind farms on their land, as wind power is considered an important renewable energy source? Is it okay for them to fight hunting bans on wolves and other predators? Is it okay for them to frame their identity in terms that might appear nationalistic? While few on the left dare to openly criticize the Sámi, these questions make many feel uncomfortable. And in a culture such as that of the Nordic countries, where avoiding uncomfortable issues often takes precedence over trying to resolve them, the consequence is that, well, they will not be resolved.

The final push to conceive this book came from a new generation of Sámi artists who combine agitprop and Sámi traditions in ways so remarkable that I felt their work and their messages needed to be recognized by the broadest audience possible. It was a spring 2018 telephone conversation with one of them, Anders Sunna, that encouraged me enough to embark on what still seemed like a daunting project.

After all, I needed to find an answer as to how I, a complete outsider, could do the topic justice. Obviously, not belonging to the Sámi community yourself puts certain restrictions on what you can do, both scholarly and ethically. The following quote by Swedish journalist Po Tidholm, an expert on the far north, also rang in my ears: "I have worked as a journalist for almost twenty years, but despite regular prompts by newspaper editors and book publishers, I have very consciously avoided to write about the Sámi. If you do, it is impossible not to mess things up. The matter is politically, historically, legally, and culturally very complex."[4]

What were my conclusions? To begin with, I will not dwell on internal conflicts and problems that the Sámi are grappling with. It is not my place to do so. The relevant discussions happen among the Sámi, and the relevant solutions will be developed by them, too.[5]

I'd like to add, however, that there is a curious assumption about conflicts among minorities. It is as if their concerns lose credibility if they do not agree on everything. What is celebrated as "democracy," "diversity," and "critical thinking" in majority culture is discredited as "turmoil," "chaos," and "immaturity" among minorities. Different Sámi have different opinions on things; that is perfectly natural. It does not make the injustice disappear that they all experience as a people, even if they disagree on how to interpret and handle that injustice. The interviewees in this book don't agree on everything, even if they all share a desire to do the best for their people. There is no contradiction here.

In terms of the book's structure, the focus lies on the voices of the Sámi artists, activists, politicians, and scholars I had the privilege to interview. Each interview is followed by a text (a document, a poem, an essay—the form varies) to illustrate some of the contents. The included photographs and works of art serve the same purpose. The introduction is intended to provide relevant background information about Sámi history and politics, while the appendix lists English-language sources that inclined readers can use to investigate further.

There are a few things I would like to clarify before I proceed.

Indigenous Peoples

This is a book about an indigenous people from the north of Europe. A philosophical discussion about what it means to be an indigenous people would require a book of its own. The working definition I am using here is based on the International Labour Organization's "Indigenous and Tribal Peoples Convention" from 1989, commonly known as ILO 169. It defines indigenous peoples as "peoples in independent countries who are regarded as indigenous on account of their descent from the populations which inhabited the country, or a geographical region to which the country belongs, at the time of conquest or colonisation or the establishment of present state boundaries and who, irrespective of their legal status, retain some or all of their own social, economic, cultural and political institutions."[6] If anyone requires a more concise and digestible definition, we can also cite the "Factsheet" of the Permanent Forum on Indigenous Issues, according to which indigenous peoples are "the descendants—according to a common definition—of those who inhabited a country or a geographical region at the time when people of different cultures or ethnic origins arrived."[7]

No one can seriously doubt the status of the Sámi as an indigenous people based on these definitions. It doesn't stop some from claiming that the Sámi "no longer live like indigenous people," as if there was any particular way of doing so. When ILO 169 speaks of retaining social, economic, cultural, and political institutions, it doesn't mean that these institutions can't change; it only means that they can be traced back to a time before the colonizers came. In this context, it is also irrelevant how much an indigenous people are suffering economically. You don't stop being indigenous if you're not dirt poor in a material sense (which the majority of indigenous people in the world are). Here is how a 2011 United Nations report put it: "Today, Sami people in the Nordic countries do not have to deal with many of the socio-economic concerns that commonly face indigenous peoples throughout the world, such as serious health concerns, extreme poverty or hunger. Norway, Sweden and Finland are among the wealthiest and most developed countries in the world and consistently rank toward the top of human development indicators."[8]

Socio-economic security is of course not the only requirement for a people's well-being. The Sámi's well-being is far from guaranteed by integration into the Nordic welfare state model, as the suffering caused by colonization is far from over. Because the Sámi are—in one way or another—recognized as an indigenous people by the governments of Norway, Sweden, Finland, and Russia, they should be granted special rights according to international agreements. The UN Declaration on the Rights of Indigenous Peoples of 2007 states: "Indigenous peoples have the right to self-determination. By virtue of that right they freely determine their political status and freely pursue their economic, social and cultural development. . . . States in consultation and cooperation with indigenous peoples, shall take the appropriate measures, including legislative measures, to achieve the ends of this Declaration."[9]

Sápmi and Sámi

The term *Sápmi* not only describes the traditional homeland of the Sámi, but also refers to the totality of Sámi culture, life, and spirituality. "Liberating Sápmi" therefore evokes the liberation not only of a territory but of a people.

When used in a geographical sense, the term "Sámiland" is sometimes used as an equivalent to "Sápmi." The area isn't clearly defined, as the Sámi never laid claim to any territory in a legal sense. The boundaries roughly correspond to the area of prolonged Sámi settlement. The maps drawn by Sámi artist Hans Ragnar Mathisen (also known as Keviselie) can be used for orientation.[10]

When referring to the Sámi areas within the nation-states of Norway, Sweden, Finland, and Russia, it is common in the Nordic languages, including Sámi, to speak of the Norwegian, Swedish, Finnish, and Russian "sides" of Sápmi. While such wording is not conventional in English, it is perfectly understandable and will be used in this book.

The term *Sámi* (also spelled "Sami" or "Saami" in English) only became commonly used in non-Sámi languages in the 1980s, when it was recognized as the preferred form of Sámi self-identification. Before that, *lapp* was the common term used in Sweden, Finland, and Russia, and *finn* in Norway, not to be confused with the term *finne*, used for a person from Finland. *Finn* as a name for the Sámi probably derived from the Norwegian verb *finna*, to find, recognizing the Sámi's excellent pathfinding skills. The word *lapp*, whose origins remain unknown, carries strong derogatory connotations. It is used as a synonym for "fool" beyond the Nordic countries— for example, in the German dialect I grew up speaking—and is today considered a racial slur. *Lapland*, however, is still the official name for the northernmost provinces of Sweden and Finland. Historically, it has been used as an imprecise term for all areas of Sámi settlement.

Representation

I have made an effort to gather a diverse group of people as contributors to this book, in terms of age, place of residence, and occupation. At the same time, it would of course be ludicrous to claim that any twelve individuals featured in a book can represent the range of opinions that exist among their people. For a broader picture of "what Sámi think," readers are encouraged to consult the sources listed in the appendix or, if it is a possibility at all, travel to Sápmi. You can also meet with Sámi at international festivals and gatherings. Personal encounters will always leave the deepest impressions.

Most of the people I approached for interviews were people whose work I knew. Some were recommended to me. Not everyone was available during the summer of 2019, when I traveled to Sápmi to conduct the interviews. Luckily, the twelve wonderful people I got to talk to were.[11]

Compared to Norway and, particularly, Sweden, I have less insight into the situation of the Sámi in Finland and Russia, since I do not speak the national languages. Luckily, English is widely spoken among the Sámi community in Finland, and several Sámi websites from the Finnish side offer news and articles in English as well. The media of the Swedish-speaking minority in Finland also carries articles about Sápmi.

The biggest challenge in terms of gathering firsthand knowledge concerned the Sámi community in Russia. Cut off from the Sámi in the Nordic countries for a long time due to the Iron Curtain, contact has improved since the collapse of the Soviet Union in 1991, but red tape remains an issue and the Kola Peninsula is the only part of Sápmi I have not been able to visit. Online communication is impeded by language barriers. The biggest problem, however, is the political situation in Russia. Because dissent has caused harsh repression in recent years, it is risky for members of minorities to publicly state things that may be seen as critical of the government. It is the main reason why no member of the Sámi community from the Kola Peninsula is among the contributors to this book. I have included as much information about the Sámi in Russia as I've been able to. The appendix contains further sources.

Romanticization

"With all due respect to those who admire the Swedes, I'd have preferred to live like a Sami," writes Marxist blogger Louis Proyect in an article on Swedish colonialism.[12] While it is easy to sympathize with the statement, it is important to note that supporting anticolonial struggles does not, in fact, require an identification with the colonized people. In other words: to support the Sámi struggle for justice is not dependent on whether you would like to live like a Sámi; it is dependent on whether you like justice.

Every nonindigenous person writing about indigenous peoples must be aware of the dangers of exotification and romanticization. The temptations of exploiting "noble savage" imagery are always lurking. Especially in well-intended accounts, indigenous people are all too easily portrayed as mythical figures in tune with nature but, alas, out of tune with the needs of the modern world.

However, sometimes accusations of exotification and romanticization come too quickly. In working with Sámi it is impossible to ignore the importance that is put on both spirituality and what is regularly referred to as the "connection to the land." One of today's most prominent Sámi activists, Jenni Laiti, has stated: "People want solutions. We have these solutions because we communicate with nature. We can interpret nature's language."[13]

Sámi history also shows a remarkable restraint when it comes to the use of force or violence. The reminder that the Sámi have no word for "war" might be overused but still indicates that central features of modern politics have no equivalent in Sámi culture. Any account trying to do the culture justice needs to recognize this.

Finally, there is no doubt that we can all learn from indigenous peoples, not least in the context of fighting for humankind's survival.[14] As one Sámi activist I talked to put it, "The Sámi could have taught us about climate change a hundred years ago. But no one cared to listen."

Names

Sápmi is a multilingual area and naming places can be confusing. Most places have several names: a Sámi one, a colonial one (meaning one in Norwegian, Swedish, Finnish, or Russian—or, particularly in border areas, two or three of them), and sometimes further ones in other minority languages such as Kven or Meänkieli. In addition, spelling differs between Sámi dialects; *Sápmi*, for example, is spelled *Sábme* in Lule Sámi and *Saepmie* in South Sámi. Many non-Sámi place names are based on the traditional Sámi name.

While it was tempting to use colonial names for places in Sápmi in this book, as they are most recognizable and traceable for an international audience (that is, they are the names you'd find on most maps), Sámi names have been used throughout. The spelling of each name corresponds to the Sámi dialect that was historically prevalent in the respective area.[15] Exceptions have been made when using established English terms that contain colonial names, such as Tromsø Airport or University of Luleå.

When using Sámi words other than place names, I consistently use North Sámi spelling, as North Sámi is the dialect used by the majority of Sámi speakers.

Photo: Gabriel Kuhn

The list on the opposite page provides the Sámi place names used in this book alongside the colonial names and the countries they are located in. Two maps of Sápmi are also included on the following pages: one with Sámi names, the other with colonial ones.

Aanaar (Aanaar Sámi)—Inari *Finland*

Áltá (North Sámi)—Alta *Norway*

Bådåddjo (Lule Sámi)—Bodø *Norway*

Bájil (North Sámi)—Pajala *Sweden*

Deanušaldi (North Sámi)—Tana Bru *Norway*

Dearna (South Sámi)—Tärnaby *Sweden*

Gállok (Lule Sámi)—Kallak *Sweden*

Gárasavvon (North Sámi)—Karesuando/Karesuvanto *Sweden/Finland*

Gáregasnjárga (North Sámi)—Karigasniemi *Finland*

Girkonjárga (North Sámi)—Kirkenes *Norway*

Giron (North Sámi)—Kiruna *Sweden*

Goaskinvággi (North Sámi)—Kjelvik *Norway*

Guovdageaidnu (North Sámi)—Kautokeino *Norway*

Jåhkåmåhke (Lule Sámi)—Jokkmokk *Sweden*

Julevu (Lule Sámi)—Luleå *Sweden*

Kárášjohka (North Sámi)—Karasjok *Norway*

Leavdnja (North Sámi)—Lakselv *Norway*

Liksjoe (Lule Sámi)—Lycksele *Sweden*

Lujávri (North Sámi)—Lovozero *Russia**

Máze (North Sámi)—Masi *Norway*

Murmánska (North Sámi)—Murmansk *Russia**

Njuorggán (North Sámi)—Nuorgam *Finland*

Ohcejohka (North Sámi)—Utsjoki *Finland*

Porsáŋgu (North Sámi)—Porsanger *Norway*

Raavrhjohke (South Sámi)—Rönnbäck *Sweden*

Roavvenjárga (North Sámi)—Rovaniemi *Finland*

Romsa (North Sámi)—Tromsö *Norway*

Sállir (North Sámi)—Kvaløya *Norway*

Snåase (South Sámi)—Snåse *Norway*

Staare (South Sámi)—Östersund *Sweden*

Šuoššjávri (North Sámi)—Suossjavri *Norway*

Suttes (Lule Sámi)—Boden *Sweden*

Tråante (South Sámi)—Trondheim *Norway*

Ubmeje (Ume Sámi)—Umeå *Sweden*

Váhtjer (Lule Sámi)—Gällivare *Sweden*

Vyöddale (Ume Sámi)—Vindeln *Sweden*

* Historically, Kildin Sámi was the main Sámi dialect spoken in the regions
of Lujávri and Murmánska. It is transcribed using Cyrillic script.

Sápmi

Sámi Dialects

1. South Sámi
2. Ume Sámi
3. Pite Sámi
4. Lule Sámi
5. North Sámi
6. Aanaar Sámi
7. Skolt Sámi
8. Kildin Sámi
9. Ter Sámi

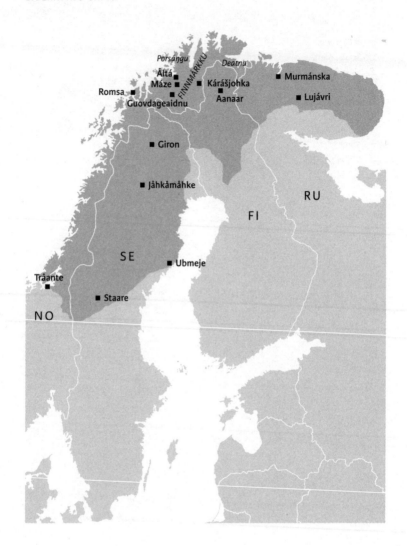

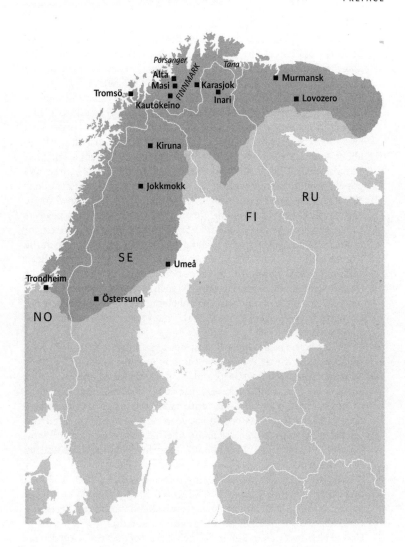

NOTES

1   There are various reasons for this. The image of the "noble savage" became popular during eighteenth-century German Romanticism. Later, sympathies for Native Americans were used for propaganda purposes by the anti-American political Right and Left alike.

2   The disinterest of the majority population has played into the hands of the Nordic governments. Their colonial policies were built to a large degree on leaving the public in the dark about the treatment of the Sámi. Some observers suggest that people in the Nordic countries know more about American Indians than about the indigenous peoples of their own countries. This depends on where these people live, of course. As a popular saying has it, people in the south of the Nordic countries don't care about the Sámi, while people in the north hate them. However, to exclusively blame the Sámi's neighbors for their mistreatment neglects the fact that all people in the far north suffer from economic exploitation, political neglect, and social prejudice. The dismantling of the Nordic welfare states deepens unresolved tensions in marginalized communities. The profits made in the north largely benefit the wealthy classes of the south. Yet activist slogans such as "Autonomt Norrland" do not provide feasible solutions. The policies of regional governments in the north have often been worse for the Sámi than those of the national governments.

3   There are some indications that things are about to change. In 2018, organizers of the anarchist book fair in Ubmeje specified in their announcement that the fair took place in "Occupied Sápmi."

4   Po Tidholm, *Norrland* (Luleå: Teg, 2014), 205. Translated by G.K.

5   Unsurprisingly, many of these conflicts are the result of colonial policies, from the legal distinction between reindeer herding Sámi and others in Sweden to debates about whether the Association of Sámi Writers in Norway should or should not include Sámi authors writing in Norwegian.

6   Quoted from https://www.ilo.org/dyn/normlex/en/f?p=NORMLEXPU B:12100:0::NO:12100:P12100_INSTRUMENT_ID:312314:NO.

7   United Nations Permanent Forum on Indigenous Issues, *Factsheet: Indigenous Peoples, Indigenous Voices* (New York, n.d.).

8   United Nations Human Rights Council, *Report of the Special Rapporteur on the Rights of Indigenous Peoples, James Arraya, Addendum: The Situation of the Sami People in Sápmi Region of Norway, Sweden, and Finland* (A/HRC/18/35/Add.2), June 6, 2011, 5.

9   United Nations, *United Nations Declaration on the Rights of Indigenous Peoples* (61/295), September 13, 2007, 8, 14.

10   A *Sámi Atlas* based on Mathisen's work was published in 1996.

11   Many people apart from those interviewed helped to realize this project. Among them are Birgitta Edeborg and Anne Bryggman-Tjikkom from Ája, the library and archive of Ájtte—the Swedish Mountain and Sámi Museum in Jåhkåmåhke, Ann-Silje Ingebrigtsen and Lena Karlstrøm

from the Alta Museum, Dirk Grosjean, Crispin Gurholt, Niillas Holmberg, Jonas Lundström, Hans Ragnar Mathisen, Cristina Ruiz-Kellersmann, Moa Sandström, Nils-Henrik Sikku, Anna Tenfält, Svante Tidholm, and Aina Tollefsen. Responsibility for the book's contents lies, of course, exclusively with me.

12 Louis Proyect, "Swedish Colonialism, Part 1: The Persecution of the Sami," July 7, 2015, www.louisproyect.org/2015/07/07/swedish-colonialism-part-1-the-persecution-of-the-sami/.

13 Quoted from Moa Sandström, "DeCo2onising Artivism," in Marianne Liliequist and Coppélie Cocq, eds., *Samisk kamp: Kulturförmedling och rättviserörelse* (Umeå: h:ström, 2017), 88. Translation by G.K.

14 There are plenty of lessons to be learned in sustainability to begin with. This takes on very concrete forms. See, for example, the *Sámi Huksendáidda* zine, edited by Sámi architect Joar Nango, which documents Sámi "do-it-yourself" (DIY) skills.

15 The historically prevalent dialect doesn't always correspond to the currently prevalent dialect. In Aanaar, for example, North Sámi speakers make up the majority of Sámi speakers today, while the town is the historical center of the Aanaar Sámi-speaking community.

INTRODUCTION

A Short Political History of Sápmi

Overview

It is hard to put exact numbers on the Sámi. The Nordic countries do not keep official statistics on ethnicity or race, and self-identification plays a significant role. It is not uncommon for families to be divided into members who identify as Sámi and others who don't. Some of the most prominent Sámi—among them, former NHL star Börje Salming and world-class skier Anja Pärson—were not known to be Sámi among the general population for a long time.

The closest we come to official definitions of Sámi identity are the regulations for those eligible to vote for the Sámi parliaments. In Norway and Sweden, one needs to self-identify as a Sámi, and at least one grandparent must be a Sámi language speaker. In Finland, the regulations are similar, but there also exists an old Sámi population register. In Russia, there is no direct popular vote for the Sámi Parliament; its members are delegated by Sámi organizations.

The numbers of registered voters in the latest Sámi parliament elections were 16,958 in Norway (2017), 8,766 in Sweden (2017), and 5,873 in Finland (2019). However, there are both Sámi speakers who don't register as Sámi parliament voters, and self-identified Sámi who don't qualify given the regulations. The 2011 United Nations report on the Sámi gave the following numbers, albeit without citing sources: "The Sami population is estimated to be between 70,000 and 100,000, with about 40,000–60,000 in Norway, about 15,000–20,000 in Sweden, about 9,000 in Finland and about 2,000 in Russia."[1] The website samer.se, the online presence of the Sámi Information Center in Sweden, lists similar numbers: Norway 50,000–65,000, Sweden 20,000–40,000, Finland ca. 8,000, Russia ca. 2,000.[2]

Sámi often distinguish themselves from "Norwegians," "Swedes," "Finns," or "Russians," who are frequently referred to as "neighbors." How Sámi interpret the fact that they are citizens of Norway, Sweden, Finland, or Russia varies. For some, these identities are not mutually exclusive, and they consider themselves to be as much Norwegian, Swedish, Finnish, or Russian as they consider themselves to be Sámi. Others do not consider themselves to be part of majority society in any way.

In political discourse, this can create confusion, especially in the context of far-right politics where cultural and national identities often are conflated. In 2014, Björn Söder, a high-ranking member of the Sweden Democrats, stated that the country's recognized minorities, including the Sámi, did not belong to the Swedish nation. In the discussions that followed, some Sámi, despite objecting to Söder's politics, said that the statement itself was correct: Sámi are indeed not Swedes. The problem here is that the "Swedish nation" is but a political construct without any particular cultural identity, no matter how much right-wingers try to construe one. The construction only serves to exclude certain people from citizenship or, where this is not possible such as in the case of the Sámi, to suggest that they are "lesser" citizens, with all the problematic implications this entails. While a distinction between Sámi and Swedes, to stick to the above example, makes sense on a colloquial level, it does not make sense in political discourse, where cultural identity and citizenship are two different things. On that level, Sámi are as Swedish as anyone else holding a Swedish passport, and it is shameful for politicians to suggest otherwise.

While self-identification and language are key criteria for the Sámi parliament definitions of whom to consider a Sámi, Swedish law includes another criterion, namely owning and herding reindeer. The latter is a requirement for membership in a *sameby*, an economic association of reindeer-herding families. While individual Sámi have no special rights in Sweden, *samebyar* do. In other words, the law divides the country's Sámi into two classes. This has caused much strife within the Sámi community and continues to do so today.

Reindeer-herding Sámi make up less than 10 percent of the Sámi population on all sides of Sápmi. In absolute numbers, there are about six thousand of them, caring for half a million reindeer. Given the significance of the reindeer in Sámi history and mythology, reindeer herders are often seen as "keepers of the tradition," the ones to maintain Sámi culture in its purest form. But while the reindeer is without doubt strongly associated with Sámi culture, many Sámi persistently point out that one does not need to own reindeer to be Sámi, and that there have always been Sámi who haven't.[3]

Traditional Sámi society is often divided into four groups:

- The *Mountain Sámi* define the popular image of the Sámi. They keep big herds of reindeer and accompany them on long journeys between seasonal pastures. On a single trip, they can cover up to a thousand kilometers. In 2017, the Norwegian public broadcaster NRK provided a 168-hour livestream of reindeer migration from Šuoššjávri to Sállir.

- The *Forest Sámi* keep their reindeer in forested areas. The reindeer migrate to new pastures during the year, but distances aren't as vast as among Mountain Sámi. Forest Sámi often supplement reindeer herding with other forms of income: agriculture, hunting, fishing, and handicraft production.

- The *Sea Sámi*, the most numerous of the commonly defined Sámi groups, live along the northern coast of Norway. Their traditional livelihood consists of fishing in the Norwegian and Barents Seas. They were the first Sámi to trade with outsiders.

- The *River Sámi* are predominantly salmon fishers along the Deatnu River. They make up a few thousand people.

While these categories help to get a rough overview of traditional Sámi society, the majority of Sámi today don't fall into any of them.[4] Far more than half of today's Sámi live in urban areas where they engage in professions that don't differ from those of the rest of the population. While derogatory terms such as "asphalt Sámi" have been used to ridicule them, they are today a strong and respected part of Sámi society.[5]

As a result of the colonization of Sápmi—which included settlerism, forced migration, and assimilation policies—the Sámi are today a minority pretty much anywhere they live. Exceptions are the inner parts of Finnmark County in Norway and the municipality of Ohcejohka in Finland, just south of the Finnmark border. Towns in which Sámi constitute a majority or significant part of the population are Guovdageaidnu and Kárášjohka on the Norwegian side, Aanaar on the Finnish side, Jåhkåmåhke on the Swedish side, and Lujávri on the Russian side. Here you find Sápmi's most important administrative, cultural, and educational institutions.

Early History and Language

The origins of the Sámi people are unclear. What scholars seem to agree on is that they arrived in the region known as Fennoscandia around roughly 2000 BC coming from the east. Fennoscandia signifies the large peninsula encompassing Scandinavia, Finland, Karelia, and the Kola Peninsula. Cap of the North is a related term but limited to the parts of Fennoscandia that lie north of the Arctic Circle.

In the course of the centuries, the Sámi settled along the northern coast of modern-day Norway and went farther south. Archaeological excavations have revealed a Sámi presence at around 1000 BC in the Swedish province of Härjedalen, which lies at the Norwegian border, a mere four hundred kilometers north of Oslo.

The Sámi's Eastern origins are also confirmed by the Sámi language, which belongs to the Finno-Ugric language family whose roots lie at the Volga and Oka Rivers of Russia. Different forms of the Sámi language developed over time, eleven of them recognized by linguists. The verdict on whether they constitute Sámi dialects or separate Sámi languages is still out. As Sámi scholar Harald Gaski points out in his interview in this book, the characterization chosen often depends on whether one wants to stress Sámi unity or diversity. In an article titled "The 'White Indians' of Scandinavia," Gaski provided a very illustrative description of how the Sámi dialects (I will follow Gaski's terminological preference here) relate to one another:

> The differences between neighboring dialects, however, are so minor that mutual understanding is quite possible. For

example, a message sent from the southernmost part of Samiland can easily pass through the entire Sami area to the northernmost and easternmost parts in Sami language, with only minor adjustments from one dialect to another. But the dialects at the starting and ending points of the route will not be mutually intelligible—they will, in fact, be as far apart as Norwegian and German.[6]

Out of the eleven classified Sámi dialects, the far most widespread today is North Sámi with an estimated fifteen to twenty thousand speakers. Lule Sámi ranks second with about two thousand. All other Sámi dialects have less than a thousand speakers, some less than a hundred. Kemi Sámi and Akkala Sámi, once spoken in the eastern parts of Sápmi, are considered extinct.

The majority of Sámi today do not speak the language, but there has been a recent revival in its use. All across Sápmi there are radio and television programs in Sámi, language classes, schools, and a prolific publishing world.

Traditionally, the Sámi were a nomadic people hunting and fishing. As nomads in the Arctic region, Sámi are considered the inventors of the ski; rock paintings with depictions of Sámi hunters on skis date back several thousand years.

Reindeer were domesticated and used as working animals already before the Common Era. Only in the sixteenth century, however, did large-scale breeding and herding begin. It didn't take long before reindeer herding became a pillar of the Sámi economy and an inherent part of Sámi culture and identity.

Trading began when outsiders visited the coastal areas of Sápmi during the Viking Age (793–1066). The Sámi traded animal hides, fur, feathers, walrus teeth, and handicrafts for salt, metal blades, and coins. If it is true, as legend has it, that Harald Fairhair (ca. 850–932), Norway's first king, who unified the country, married Snøfrid, daughter of a Sámi family, it would indicate that the Sámi still held a powerful position at the time, considering the intricate world of royal marriage. A combination of cunning outside businessmen, increased government control, and taxation tipped the scale against the Sámi at the end of the Middle Ages.

In line with anthropological studies of nomads as "societies without a state," traditional Sámi society has been described as "anarchist."[7] It was based on groups of about a hundred people who roamed around a roughly defined area. North Americans are often surprised about the striking cultural parallels to American Indian cultures, which include religious and artistic practices as well as material objects of everyday use such as shamanic drums and tipi-like tents. Here is a brief overview of some key terms:

- A *siida* is the traditional form of Sámi community; the name is still used in Norway to define associations of reindeer herders.
- The *luohti* is commonly known as the yoik, a traditional form of Sámi singing, evoking (rather than reflecting on) a person or a place.
- *Duodji* is often referred to as traditional Sámi handicraft, as it concerns the production of items for everyday use (from cups and bags to clothes and knives), but Sámi scholars have pointed out that "the gathering, treatment and use of working materials (such as wood or reindeer leather) are an integral part of Sámi epistemologies and belief systems"—in this sense, "*duodji* is both the making of an item and the item itself."[8]
- The *gákti* is a traditional Sámi garment reminiscent of a vest, often multicolored and intricately designed, providing information about the wearer's social status, family, and origin; in English, it is more commonly known by the Norwegian word *kofte*, or the Swedish word *kolt*.
- A *goahti* is a traditional Sámi house, usually pyramid-shaped; it can consist of different material (fabric, peat moss, timber) and there are stationary and portable ones; the latter include the *lávvu*, which is reminiscent of a tipi.
- A *noaidi*, commonly translated as "shaman," is a traditional healer and central figure in Sámi spirituality; Sámi spirituality is commonly classified as animism, explained thus by Sámi historian Aage Solbakk: "Here in Sápmi, all of nature is alive. Everything has a soul, whether it is a birch or a rock, a lake or a creek."[9]
- A *goavddis* is a traditional Sámi drum used for ceremonial and spiritual purposes.
- A *sieidi* is a sacred site, in most cases an unconventional rock formation.

It is often said that the book *Germania*, authored by the famed Roman historian Tacitus in 98 AD, contains the first popular description of the Sámi. However, it is not entirely clear who the people referred to as "Fenni" by Tacitus are. It might be an umbrella term used for different peoples inhabiting the northeast of Europe at the time.

Certainly more accurate were the descriptions in the 1673 book *Lapponia*, penned by the German-Swedish scholar Johannes Schefferus. "Lapponia" is the Latin translation of the term *Lappland*, used for the northernmost parts of Sweden, which at the time included Finland. The area corresponds to the modern-day provinces of Swedish and Finnish Lapland. Schefferus relied heavily on information provided by Olaus Sirma, a Sámi priest and poet. The two yoiks by Sirma included in *Lapponia* were translated into several European languages and secured the author a place in European literary history.

1600–1900: Colonization and Rebellion

In 1635, mining was introduced in Sápmi when a silver mine opened near Árjepluovve in Sweden. The impact on Sámi society was huge. Businessmen and settlers arrived from the south, while local Sámi were driven from their homes and used as coolies. Resistance was met with harsh repression. A special kind of water torture became notorious: Sámi were dragged along a rope underneath the ice of a frozen lake from one hole to another. Many of them fled the area, often ending up as underpaid laborers or vagrant beggars. This is where terms such as *fattiglapp* ("poor lapp") and *lapproletariat* have their origins.

While physical oppression was an intrinsic part of the colonization of Sápmi, depriving the Sámi of both their spirituality and the material basis for their livelihoods had the most devastating effects. In 2004, Victoria Harnesk of the Sámi Association in Stockholm stated, "We, the Sámi people, have not been subject to a bloody genocide but of a cultural, 'soft' genocide, based on hidden but effective tools employed by the Swedish state to steal our land, water, language, religion, identity, and the possibility to pursue our traditional livelihoods."[10]

During the seventeenth century, the growing number of settlers, administrators, and missionaries put increasing pressure on the Sámi's traditional way of life. Settlers were enticed to move north with promises of free land and tax deductions. The price was paid by the Sámi. Christianization was ruthless, as *goavddis* were confiscated, *sieidi* destroyed, and *noaidi* burned at the stake—forty in Finnmark alone, many of them on a small island near the nowadays abandoned fishing village of Goaskinvággi.

In the eighteenth century, colonial structures were firmly in place in Sápmi. Forced dislocation and what is known today as "land grabbing" had become common practice, both to create space for the continued arrival of settlers, to take control of the waterways, and to establish industries exploiting the region's natural resources, mainly minerals and timber. Sámi who resisted dislocation had their fences torn down and reindeer killed by settlers coming from the south. An anecdote related by author Helena Carlsson tells about a collision of perspectives that has not disappeared to this day:

> One winter day, a substitute teacher came to a school in the municipality of Vyöddale. He was one of many who commuted from Ubmeje to one of the Vyöddale schools. He was angry and upset because he had arrived late for his very first day at work, having been delayed by a herd of reindeer. When it was time for the first break of the day, his anger still hadn't subsided. He sat on a chair in the teachers' room and wondered loudly why reindeer always had to be right where cars were supposed to drive. Everyone in the room fell silent, since almost all of the other teachers knew that one of them was a reindeer owner herself. Calmly, she said, "I wonder why they always have to build roads right where we have our best pastures."[11]

The anecdote also reminds us of how cunning the language of politicians can be. As it has become popular for politicians in the Nordic countries to present themselves as protectors of minorities, including the Sámi, their support for development in mining, infrastructure, hydroelectricity, and wind power, is often justified by pretexts such as "there is a place for everything." The problem is: there isn't. If politicians are serious about protecting Sámi culture, they must choose and prioritize.

In the 1750s, natural developments also affected the Sámi negatively. An overpopulation of reindeer and the sudden increase in the population of wolves led to thousands of reindeer being killed. In the region of Jåhkåmåhke, two thirds of the reindeer population perished.

Christianity had by now become dominant among the Sámi. However, many Sámi had adopted a double religious life: while they officially accepted Christianity and attended church services, they often maintained shunned traditional practices in secrecy.

The first open Sámi rebellion emerged from a Pietist Sámi-Christian revival movement instigated by the priest Lars Levi Læstadius in the 1830s. Læstadius, himself of Sámi descent, was well-versed in Sámi mythology and used his knowledge to reach a Sámi audience, ironically turning his followers against central aspects of Sámi culture, including the yoik. The success of Læstadius advocating abstinence, anti-worldliness, and repentance is largely attributed to the state of disarray that had encompassed Sámi society at the time. The moral consensus that had held Sámi society together for centuries had been undermined, reindeer theft was a common occurrence, and many Sámi had fallen victim to alcoholism. Læstadius's promise to not only escape misery through adherence to a strict moral code but to also form a vanguard of righteousness able to purify what was considered a world of sin appealed to a small but enthusiastic Sámi minority. With respect to Sámi identity, Læstadianism was a double-edged sword: while effectively eradicating certain parts of the Sámi tradition, it also provided many Sámi with a sense of pride and self-respect.

Læstadian communities remain to this day, in Sápmi and beyond. There is disagreement on the value of Læstadianism for the development of Sámi culture. It is clear, however, that Læstadianism inspired the Sámi who rebelled in Guovdageaidnu in 1852, an event described by Sámi historians as "part of a wider global history of conflictive contact between Indigenous and colonial forces."[12]

Læstadian Sámi in the Guovdageaidnu region had started to show disobedience to Norwegian authorities, including the Church of Norway, some years prior to the events. They were pronounced critics of commercial interests holding sway over Sápmi and, in particular, the trade with alcohol. After repeated confrontations with clerics, several Sámi were imprisoned. Tensions rose steadily.

On November 8, 1852, a group of about fifty rebellious Sámi went to Guovdageaidnu to set an example. They killed the merchant Carl Johan Ruth and the government agent Lars Johan Bucht before they were overwhelmed by residents of the town and made prisoners. In January 1853, they were brought to trial. Two alleged leaders, Aslak Jacobsen Hætta and Mons Aslaksen Somby, were executed, about twenty others sentenced to forced labor between eight months and life. By 1867, all of them had been pardoned and released.

The Guovdageaidnu events spread awareness about the problems of the Sámi in the Nordic countries. This led to an era of benevolence among the upper classes, while the everyday oppression of the Sámi on the ground continued.

One of the consequences was a fate shared by many oppressed and impoverished people of Europe at the time: emigration. A few hundred Sámi took the opportunity to move to Alaska when help with the introduction of reindeer herding was needed in the late 1890s.[13] Others joined the general wave of migrant laborers from the Nordic countries to the so-called New World. Today, the number of descendants of Sámi immigrants in North America is estimated at thirty thousand.[14] Some of them are organized in associations such as Pacific Sámi Searvi in Washington State (searvi is the Sámi word for "association") and the Sámi Cultural Center of North America.[15] Celebrities reputed to have Sámi ancestry include singer Joni Mitchell and actress Renée Zellweger.

The Twentieth Century: Nation-States and Sámi Organizing

The national borders drawn across Sápmi changed several times throughout the centuries, with Danish, Norwegian, Swedish, and Russian royals controlling shifting parts of territory. The borders divided families, cut off pastures, and introduced bureaucracy alien to Sámi culture. At times, Sámi were forced to pay taxes to three rulers, as they were regularly crossing borders with their reindeer. In 1751, the Lapp Codicil was signed; sometimes referred to as the "Sámi's Magna Carta," it was the first document to recognize special Sámi rights with regard to border crossings and reindeer herding.

The union of the Sámi across the national borders most of them deem artificial is emphasized to this day. Yet the national borders have also created particular conditions for the Sámi living in the different nation-states. National languages, codes of law, education systems, and cultural traits have all impacted the respective Sámi communities.

Today's borders were established in the early part of the twentieth century. Norway became independent from Sweden in 1905, Finland from Russia in 1917. With the Russian Revolution of the same year and the Iron Curtain, the Sámi on the Kola Peninsula were essentially cut off from the Sámi communities in the Nordic countries, spending almost a century in isolation. This changed after the Soviet Union's fall in 1991. Two years later, the Norwegian Barents Secretariat was established in Girkonjárga, close to the Russian border. One of its purposes was to strengthen the relationship to the Sámi community on the Russian side.

In the early twentieth century, the Sámi were subjected to a particularly hideous form of abuse, justified in the name of science: racial biology. This was especially pronounced in Sweden, where, in 1922, the State Institute for Racial Biology was established at Uppsala University, the country's oldest and most prestigious. The institute existed until 1958.

Swedish officials—Social Democrats included—were keen adherents of this new (pseudo)scientific discipline. Medical staff was sent to Sápmi to measure Sámi skulls and bones. Sámi students had their pictures taken under humiliating circumstances, being forced to undress in front of their teachers, peers, and medical staff. Sámi skulls and skeletons were transferred to research facilities and museums. Racial biology didn't stop at "collecting data," however. For decades, the National Swedish Board of Health enforced the compulsory sterilization of women deemed improper to have children. The laws underpinning this practice were only abolished in 1976.[16] While the Sámi were not the main target of the program, they were among the victims, in particular Sámi women.

During the heyday of racial biology, Sweden also adopted the "Sámi shall be Sámi" policy (*lapp skall vara lapp*). It was based on the assumption that, as a different race, the Sámi were incapable of being assimilated into Swedish society and should therefore be kept apart and dedicate themselves exclusively to reindeer herding. "Nomad schools" were established for Sámi children,

Decree issued by the Swedish king for settlement in Sápmi, 1673.

Top: copper carving depicting a *noadi* with his *goavddis*, eighteenth century (Wikimedia Commons). Bottom: *siedi* near Romsa (Labongo/Wikimedia Commons).

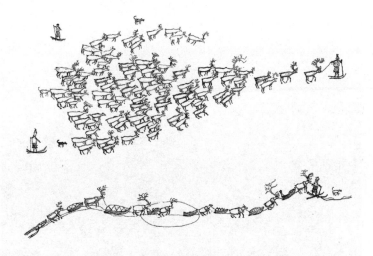

Johan Turi (1854–1936) was a Sámi reindeer herder, writer, and artist. His book *Muitalus sámiid birra* (1910) is considered the first-ever secular work published in the Sámi language. Here are depictions of a reindeer caravan (top) and the gathering of reindeer during the marking of the calves (bottom, both Wikimedia Commons).

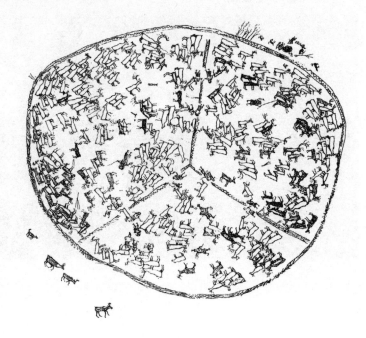

Top: milking of reindeer, ca. 1913 (National Archives of Norway). Bottom: romantic depiction of Sámi life by Norwegian painter Wilhelm Peters, ca. 1900 (National Library of Norway).

Left: Sámi mother with children. Image by Swedish photographer Borg Mesch (1869–1956) for *National Geographic* 31, no. 6, 1917. Bottom: "Nomad School" Čohkkiras/ Jukkasjärvi on the Swedish side of Sápmi, 1939 (Nordic Museum, Stockholm).

Top: Sámi reindeer herder, 2005 (Mats Andersson/Wikimedia Commons).
Bottom: Máze, 2019 (Gabriel Kuhn).

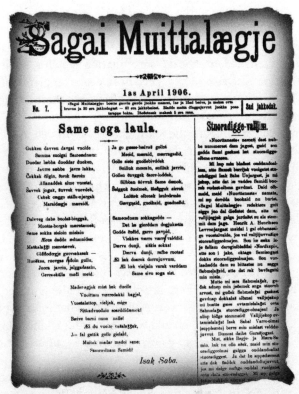

Sagai Muittalægje (The News Reporter), published from 1904 to 1911, is commonly referred to as the first Sámi political newspaper. On April 1, 1906, Isak Saba's poem "Same soga laula" ("Sámi soga lávlla" in modern North Sámi spelling) was published on the front page. In 1986, the words were adopted as the lyrics of the official Sámi anthem.

allowing them to travel with their reindeer-herding parents. What might appear as a policy respecting the Sámi's particular needs meant complete exclusion of the Sámi from mainstream society and deepened the gap between reindeer-herding Sámi and others. The policy was abandoned in the 1940s.

The governments of Norway and Finland always focused on assimilation. The prime goal of Sámi education was to detach Sámi children from traditional ways and turn them into good citizens of modern nation-states. In Norway, the term "Norwegianization" was commonly used. Sámi children were forced to attend boarding schools, sometimes only able to meet with their parents twice a year. They were punished when caught speaking Sámi.

Assimilated or not, the Sámi suffered widespread structural discrimination in education, work, and housing throughout the twentieth century. While, today, most discriminatory legislation has been abolished, practical discrimination remains, not least in health services, where Sámi experience a near-complete disregard for their own healing traditions and often only meet halfhearted responses to their problems.[17]

In order to confront the many challenges forced upon them, Sámi began to organize in the early twentieth century. Elsa Laula, born in Dearna in 1877, emerged as a prominent leader. She was a driving force behind one of the first Sámi organizations, Sweden's *Lapparnas Centralförbund* (The Central Association of Lapps), founded in 1904. Laula envisioned a pan-Sámi movement reaching beyond the colonial borders forced upon her people. In her famous 1904 treatise *Inför lif eller död* (Facing Life or Death), she wrote: "The Lapps need to take things into their own hands. 'In what way?', many ask. There is only one: to build a united Lapp association that plants roots everywhere within the Lapp population. . . . To you, young men and women, I will say one thing: the future of our people lies in your hands! With your strength, our people and our land shall persevere."[18]

In 1917, Laula organized the first Sámi National Assembly in Tråante, on the Norwegian side of Sápmi. This was a pivotal event in the history of Sámi organizing. The date of the meeting, February 6, is today celebrated as the Sámi's official national day. The assembly of Tråante was followed by one in Staare, on the Swedish side, one year later. Elsa Laula's portrait is ever-present in Sápmi to this day, adorning artwork, posters, and graffitied walls.

On the Kola Peninsula in Russia, the situation of the Sámi improved somewhat right after the revolution of 1917. Guided by the anti-imperialist principle of "national self-determination," Lenin and the Bolsheviks passed decrees to protect the Sámi's traditional ways and grant them a certain level of autonomy. This changed drastically during the purges of the Stalin era. Since Sámi on the Russian side still maintained relationships to relatives in Finland and, on occasion, crossed the border with their reindeer, they were quickly suspected to be spies and traitors. In 1937, sixty-eight of them were rounded up and driven away in police trucks. Their families never heard from them again. Only decades later

Photograph from the 1917 Sámi National Assembly in Tråante. Elsa Laula second from left (Hilfling-Rasmussen/NTNU UB).

was it made official that all of them had been executed. They were rehabilitated in 1988.

The rest of the Sámi on the Russian side fell victim to forced collectivization and relocation. The majority of them settled in the small town of Lujávri. Programs to help them maintain Sámi traditions, including their language, were not available for decades.

During World War II, Sámi—even family members—were pitted against one another by the warring powers. The German army, which had occupied Norway, stood at the Soviet border in Finnmark, while Finland was fighting for independence. All parties employed Sámi as guides and used their reindeer to transport equipment.[19]

With German defeat approaching, the Germans applied a scorched-earth policy in Finnmark, hoping to halt the advance of the Soviets. They burned the settlements of the entire county—an area the size of Denmark—to the ground. Almost the entire population evacuated to other parts of Norway, with only a few hundred people hiding out in remote self-made shelters. The Norwegian government had no immediate interest in repopulating Finnmark

Buildings hosting the Sámi parliaments in Kárášjohka, Norway (left, Gabriel Kuhn); Lujávri, Russia (top right, Sidik iz PTU/Wikimedia Commons); and Aanaar, Finland (bottom right, Gabriel Kuhn). Sessions of the Sámi Parliament in Sweden are held at different locations; in 2019 it was decided to build a permanent site in Staare.

after the war, being more interested in the exploitation of the territory's natural resources and its strategic military location. However, the officials were unable to stop the return of the county's inhabitants and their efforts in rebuilding their homes and communities.

Sámi organizing continued after World War II. Among the most influential new organizations were Samii Litto (Sámi Union) in Finland, founded in 1945, Norske Reindriftsamers Landsforbund (The National Association of Reindeer-Herding Sámi in Norway), founded in 1947, and Svenska Samernas Riksförbund (The National Association of Sámi in Sweden), founded in 1950. In 1956, the Nordic Sámi Council was founded as an organization uniting the Sámi of Norway, Sweden, and Finland.[20] In 1992, Sámi representatives from Russia also joined and "Nordic" was dropped from the name. The work of the Sámi Council has always been closely tied to the Sámi Conferences bringing together delegates from Sámi organizations every two to four years since 1953.

Often regarded as the first transnational indigenous organization, the Sámi Council has been very influential in pushing

Sámi rights and interests. It has paved the way for institutional changes in the nation-states occupying Sápmi and was a driving force behind the establishment of the national Sámi parliaments in Finland (1973), Norway (1989), Sweden (1993), and Russia (2010). In the early days, the Sámi institutions were often underfunded. As the late Ingwar Åhrén, first chairman of the Sámi Parliament in Sweden, liked to tell, there wasn't even a telephone in his office.

While funding may no longer be a main problem of the parliaments, jurisdiction is. None of their resolutions are binding. Legislation over Sápmi remains in the hands of the nation-state governments. The Sámi parliaments are only granted advisory roles. Ingwar Åhrén concluded at the end of his ten-year chairmanship, "It would be wrong to say that the Sámi Parliament has actual power."[21] This, of course, does not diminish the representative role of the parliaments and their function as a forum for Sámi debate.

Reindeer herding changed dramatically in the 1960s with motorization, especially the introduction of the snowmobile. Until then, Sámi reindeer herders covered enormous distances on skis, pulling sleds with the help of their animals. The snowmobile has not only made traveling much easier, it has also allowed for more permanent housing among reindeer herders, as they can reside farther away from the pastures. Helicopters are used to bring in supplies and helping hands during the marking of the calves and other labor-intensive periods. Mobile phones and global positioning systems have also impacted the reindeer-herding profession. Nonetheless, reindeer herding remains hard work in remote and treacherous areas.

This, however, was never a big concern for reindeer herders compared to the colonial powers' intrusion into their lands. Sápmi experienced a hydroelectric power boom after World War II. Dams made large areas unsuitable for reindeer herding. They also altered waterways, which are essential for the Sámi, both as freshwater sources, fishing grounds, and travel routes. In Sweden, thirteen hydroelectric power stations have been built since 1951 along the Lule River alone, which runs through the heartland of Sápmi.

In 1968, plans were presented for a hydroelectric power station along the Áltá-Guovdageaidnu River on the Norwegian side of Sápmi, including a dam that would have led to the submergence of the entire village of Máze—only the church tower would have remained visible. After much resistance, these particular plans were scrapped, but the construction of a power station along the river remained on the agenda.

1979–1982: The Álta Conflict

When, in the mid-1970s, the Norwegian government presented its altered plans for realizing the project, a resistance movement emerged whose breadth and commitment caught everyone by surprise. The catalog of a 2018 exhibition about the events, titled *Let the River Flow*, summarized the movement thus: "The People's Action against the Áltá-Gouvdageaidnu Waterway . . . radically shook the course of history in the Nordic region. . . . It grew from an unexpectedly broad movement of solidarity across civil society—Sami, Norwegian and international."[22]

As the last sentence suggests, the protests were not exclusively carried by Sámi, and they didn't only address Sámi issues either, even if they instigated a strong Sámi civil rights movement. The Áltá protest movement brought indigenous activists and their allies together with environmentalists, fishers, and concerned locals.

A leading force in the protests was the activist group Folkeaksjonen (People's Action), founded in 1978. When the group delivered a petition against the power station with fifteen thousand names to the Norwegian Parliament in November 1978, 61 percent of the people living in the municipalities of Áltá and Guovdageaidnu had signed it. The Norwegian MPs, however, were unimpressed and backed the government's plan. Ministers ridiculed the protests, suggesting that it all came down to the question of whether "the Sámi wanted to have lights in their homes or not." It didn't help much to ease the tension.

The Áltá movement emerged at a time when traditional Sámi clothing was forbidden in Oslo restaurants and racial slurs directed at Sámi were common among Swedish MPs.[23] But for those who paid attention, there had been indications that things were about to change. Sámi scholars such as Israel Ruong had entered academia, young Sámi filled the ranks of universities and art schools, and the Sámi writer, musician, and artist Nils-Aslak

Nils-Aslak Valkeapää (left) during the World Council of Indigenous Peoples conference in Giron, 1977 (photographer unknown/Lásságámmi Foundation).

Valkeapää had emerged as an important public figure advocating the rights of his people.

Another important factor, not least for the attention that the Áltá protests received globally, was the international organization of indigenous peoples initiated in the 1970s. In 1975, the World Council of Indigenous Peoples (WCIP) was founded at a conference in Port Alberni on Vancouver Island in British Columbia. Sámi activists assumed a central role in the WCIP and organized a second conference in Giron in 1977. According to Harald Gaski, these organizational efforts marked a "transition from tradition into becoming modern internationalists."[24] Buffy Sainte-Marie was among the supporters visiting the Áltá protest camp, and Winona LaDuke and Julie Felix organized solidarity campaigns in North America.

The Áltá protest camp had been established in 1979, at a place referred to as "Nullpunktet" (literally, Point Zero), along the road to where the power station was to be built. People held their ground for several months, defying police attempts to clear the road and freezing temperatures in winter.

The protests took a new turn when they were extended to Oslo. On October 8, 1979, Sámi activists erected a *lávvu* outside of the parliament building, and, after an unsuccessful meeting with Prime Minister Odvar Nordli, seven of them went on hunger strike.[25] The strike ended a week later, when Nordli promised a new parliamentary investigation into the matter and to hold construction in Áltá. The government only bought time, however. Without significant changes in its design, work on the project resumed in late 1980. When the camp at Nullpunktet was reestablished, six hundred police were housed in Áltá on a passenger ferry; they cleared the camp on January 14, arresting nine hundred people, all of whom would later be fined; Sámi from the Swedish and Finnish sides were deported.

The focus of the protests shifted once again to Oslo: on January 23, 1981, five Sámi began another hunger strike. On February 6, fourteen Sámi women from Finnmark met with the recently appointed prime minister Gro Harlem Brundtland in her office. When Brundtland abruptly left the meeting and did not return despite promises to do so, the women refused to leave. Police escorted them out of the office the next morning.

The hunger strike lasted until February 24, with three of the hunger strikers having traveled to Stockholm to avoid being force-fed by Norwegian authorities. When the strike ended, no concessions had been made.

Protests in Áltá continued until December 1981. In January 1982, Folkeaksjonen disbanded. Years of struggle had taken their toll. On February 26, 1982, the Supreme Court of Norway upheld the government's decision to build a hydroelectric power station along the Áltá-Guovdageaidnu River.

On March 20, 1982, three activists decided to make a last stand by bombing a bridge leading to the construction site. The homemade bomb they carried on their snowmobiles could have only done minor damage. When they arrived at the bridge, one of them noticed that the bomb's timer was no longer working and suspected a frozen battery. As Niillas Somby proceeded to change it, the device went off. Somby was catapulted through the air and severely injured. He would lose an eye and an arm. His companion John Reier Martinsen took him to hospital; both were arrested. The third man disappeared and remains unknown to this day.

Somby and Martinsen were charged with arson, facing twenty-one-year sentences. Somby managed to escape to Canada, where he was sheltered by First Nations for two years. He returned to Norway after the charges against him and Martinsen had been reduced to "attempt at serious damage to public property." Both were sentenced to prison terms they had already served while awaiting trial.

Martinsen was killed in a suspicious snowmobile hit-and-run while driving his dogsled in 1986.

In 1987, the Áltá hydroelectric power station opened.

A New Sámi Movement Emerges

Despite missing their goal, to halt the construction of the Áltá-Guovdageaidnu River power station, the Áltá protests are generally regarded as a success, especially in the history of the Sámi civil rights struggle. They—quite literally—put Sápmi on the map. The protests brought attention to the plight of the Sámi and caused unprecedented media interest in their situation. A community that had largely been considered passive, or even nonexistent, had emerged as a self-confident player on the political scene. As author Björn Forseth put it, "The battle over the Áltá River was lost, but the war was won."[26]

The self-identification of the Sámi as an indigenous people has been very clear in their political agitation since the 1970s. Many Sámi distinguish themselves from "Western," "European," and "white" culture, and it is commonplace to speak of "colonization" with respect to Sámi history; one doesn't have to be a political radical to do so. In fact, the colonizers themselves have used related terms. In the early seventeenth century, Sweden's Lord High Chancellor Axel Oxenstierna declared: "I don't need colonies. I have the north!"[27]

In 1969, the anthology *Nordisk nykolonialisme* (Nordic Neocolonialism) analyzed the Sámi struggle in the context of anticolonial struggles worldwide. In addressing the situation of the Sámi, it referred to the writings and actions of men such as Mahatma Gandhi, Jawaharlal Nehru, Jomo Kenyatta, Julius Nyerere, Marcus Garvey, and Malcolm X. One contributor, Per Otnes, wrote: "Inner colonies are now reaching national self-consciousness the world over, not just in the USA but also in Scotland, the Basque Country, and other parts of Spain and France."[28]

The affinity felt with other indigenous peoples also became clear in the adoption of the term "Fourth World," which was increasingly used for indigenous peoples at the time. It frequently appears in Sámi writing to this day. Ann-Kristin Håkansson, a contributor to this book, belongs to an indigenous peoples' solidarity group called Fjärde Världen, "Fourth World" in Swedish. Other indigenous peoples, especially Native Americans, have been referenced by Sámi in various ways. Examples include the 2007 book *Bury My Heart at Udtjajaure* by Udtja Lasse and the 2016 art project *Pile o'Sápmi* by Máret Ánne Sara.[29]

The newspaper *Charta 79* epitomized the combination of Sámi activists identifying with both indigenous peoples and broad civil rights struggles; it was subtitled "Newspaper for Indigenous Issues," with the main title referencing the Czechoslovakian civil rights movement Charta 77. *Charta 79* was a big success. The first issue had a print run of 150,000. Ande Somby, one of the editors, stated in a 2018 interview:

> It was started because we realized that there were so many forces against the hunger strike action of 1979. The parliament, the government, the courts, the Norwegian press—all the central institutions were very hostile. We had some supportive statements coming from here and there, and there were some friendly photographers that were documenting the actions that were happening on the lawns of the parliament. We had hoped that the Norwegian press would be supportive of the cause, but since they weren't, we realized we must start our own newspaper.[30]

The abbreviation "ČSV" became an important means of self-identification for Sámi activists. It served as an acronym open to interpretation. Variants included *Čohkke Sámiid Vuitui* ("Organize the Sámi for victory") and *Čállet Sámi Verddet* ("Write, Sámi friends!"). *Čájet Sámi Vuoiŋŋa* (roughly, "Show Sámi spirit") was the most common, however. Regardless of one's preferred interpretation, the letters stand for Sámi self-awareness, pride, the promotion of Sámi language and culture, and the fight for Sámi rights and justice.

The cultural aspects of the Sámi struggle were always very important. The five-day 1979 Davvi Šuvva Festival in Gárasavvon, bringing together indigenous musicians from around the world, has sometimes been referred to as the "Woodstock of the North."[31] Harald Gaski writes: "The Sami political awakening was, first and foremost, culturally based. The driving force behind political engagement was directed at insuring the rights to Sami language and culture. Not until later did the issue of rights to land and water come to the fore."[32]

Knut Johnsen, Sámi activist from Deatnu, wearing a ČSV T-shirt, 1974 (Hans Ragnar Mathisen).

Of particular importance in this context was the establishment of the Máze Group, a collective of seven young Sámi artists established in the village of Máze in 1978. Some of them, such as Synnøve Persen and Britta Marakatt-Labba, would later rise to international fame. Originally conceived to promote artistic production in Sápmi, the group soon found itself caught in the middle of the Áltá conflict.

Meanwhile, a movement of *Sámáidahttan* (Sámification) countered the policies of assimilation. There is an anecdote that circulates in the Stockholm art world: When it became fashionable to buy Sámi art in the 1970s, a Stockholm-based curator arranged for a meeting at the Sámi Folk High School in Jåhkåmåhke. After traveling a thousand kilometers north, he met with two art teachers who refused to speak Swedish. The curator returned home frustrated and empty-handed. I don't know how much truth there is to the story, but it still being told proves the extent to which the new Sámi self-confidence shook the cultural establishment at the time.

The Sámi never had much support from the institutionalized Left. Nordic social democracy was based on notions of progress and modernity. The Sámi seemed to stand in the way of a development that promised to make the Nordic countries better for everyone—except the Sámi. Trade unions were strong players in the mining, hydroelectricity, and forest industries of the far north, and in my conversations with participants in the Áltá protests, the Norwegian Social Democrats were described as the "most anti-Sámi" during the conflict.

The situation was somewhat different among the Far Left. In particular, projects with a pronounced anti-imperialist agenda were keen to show support. *Charta 79*, for example, was printed by the press of *Klassekampen* (Class Struggle), a radical leftist daily. John Reier Martinsen, who was involved in the ill-fated bombing that left Niillas Somby injured, was a high-ranking member of the Maoist Workers' Communist Party. In the Norwegian Parliament, the most ardent supporters of the Sámi came from the Socialist Left Party. In Sweden, Maoist publisher Oktoberförlag presented an analysis of the Sámi's plight in the country in the 1977 booklet *Samerna i Sverige* (The Sámi in Sweden). Author Göran Lundin wrote, "It is a duty for the communist movement not to leave the Sámi question to reactionaries who profit from their oppression."[33]

What left-wing radicals and Sámi activists shared throughout the 1980s was the experience of state surveillance. This has been documented in an excellent book by Lars Martin Hjorthol, *Alta: Kraftkampen som utfordret statens makt* (Áltá: The Struggle That Challenged the Power of the State, 2006), which, unfortunately for an international audience, is only available in Norwegian.

The support that the Sámi received was certainly welcome, but their struggle was driven by themselves. The Sámi civil rights movement was full of self-confidence and achieved one important symbolic step after another. In 1986, an official Sámi anthem and a flag were adopted by the Sámi Conference. The lyrics of the anthem were based on the poem "Sámi soga lávlla" (roughly, "Song of the Sámi People"), written by the Sámi teacher and politician Isak Saba in 1906. The flag was designed by Sámi artist Astrid Båhl, strongly resembling a Sámi flag designed by Máze Group member Synnøve Persen a decade earlier. In 1992, the Sámi Conference declared February 6 to be Sámi National Day, in commemoration of the 1917 Sámi National Assembly in Tråante. The Sámi Grand Prix, modeled after the Eurovision Song Contest, was introduced in 1990. Sámi sports championships, including competitions in lasso throwing, reindeer racing, and cross-country running, also became increasingly popular. Today, there is a Sámi national football team, which hosted the first World Football Cup of the Confederation of Independent Football Associations (CONIFA) in Staare in 2014. The same year, the first Sápmi Pride festival was held in Giron.

Government response from the colonial powers has been slow but forthcoming, particularly in Norway. The Norwegian government is the only one that has ratified the ILO Convention 169 (in 1990). In 1997, King Harald traveled to the Sámi Parliament to apologize "on behalf of the state for the injustice committed against the Sámi people through its harsh policy of Norwegianization."[34] In 2005, the Finnmark Act was passed, which involves the Sámi population of Finnmark in administering the territory. Strikingly, it took until 2007 before Sámi flags were welcome on Norway's national day celebrations.

Norway is also the country where the Sámi are most integrated into national politics. The first Sámi member of parliament was the abovementioned Isak Saba, elected on a Social Democratic ticket in 1906. Helga Pedersen became the first known minister of Sámi descent in 2005, heading the Ministry of Fisheries and Coastal Affairs. The national Norwegian parties also have Sámi chapters in the Sámi Parliament, including members of the right-wing Progress Party, whose main agenda is, somewhat ironically, to abolish the Sámi Parliament.

A similar presence of mainstream political parties, for better or worse, does not exist in the other Sámi parliaments. In Sweden, the Sámi parties mainly represent interest groups (reindeer herders, Forest Sámi, and so on); in Finland, individual delegates are elected in voting districts; and in Russia, delegates are appointed by Sámi organizations.

Contemporary Challenges

While the Áltá conflict and the subsequent emergence of a Sámi civil rights movement has significantly changed the position of the Sámi vis-à-vis the colonial powers, numerous challenges remain.

Racism

Anti-Sámi racism persists.[35] Particularly vulgar forms—such as bumper stickers saying "Save a Wolf, Shoot a Sámi"—might be

rare, but Sámi see themselves confronted with anti-Sámi prejudice on a regular basis. This can take the form of racial slurs, bullet
holes in Sámi town signs, or people cutting off the ears of reindeer
killed in traffic accidents in order to prevent Sámi owners from
claiming government compensation. A 2018 study by Vaartoe, the
Center for Sámi Research at Umeå University, concluded that two
thirds of Sámi living in Sweden experience racist discrimination.[36]
In Norway, Sámi actor Sverre Porsanger caused a stir when he
suggested in a 2013 TV interview that one is bound to get beat up
wearing traditional Sámi clothing in coastal Finnmark towns on
a Saturday night. In the summer of 2019, prominent Sámi artist
Britta Marakatt-Labba told listeners to a Swedish radio program
that she had just recently been called a *lappjävel* (a derogatory
term for Sámi in Swedish) by a woman in a laundromat.

In some parts of Sápmi, it is difficult to flip through local
newspapers without finding a story about legal twists, or physical confrontations, between Sámi and non-Sámi. Many of the
obstacles that Sámi face in their everyday lives still relate to a
social climate that Norwegian physician Per Fugelli, who worked
in Sápmi for several years, described in a 1981 article thus:

> The high number of Norwegians in Finnmark who hold
> racial prejudices against the Sámi is worrisome. When I say
> racial prejudices, I mean preconceived notions that all Sámi
> possess a range of innate and unchangeable negative quali-
> ties: they are lazy, demanding, stupid, unreliable, thievish,
> dirty, and prone to be drunks. . . .
>
> Another racist assumption is that the Sámi are blessed
> by the Norwegian system. But the language, the rules, the
> bureaucracy—all of it is obscure and alien to them. The
> Norwegians, on the other hand, are socialized in this system
> from day one. No wonder the Sámi lose out.
>
> Let me give you a few examples of how these preju-
> dices express themselves in everyday life: there is the con-
> tempt with which the supermarket cashier reacts to Sámi
> who have difficulties understanding the amount of money
> they owe; there are the local comedy shows that endlessly
> ridicule Sámi speaking Norwegian; there are the letter
> sections in local newspapers, where people suggest that

Fredag 18. april 1980 (11)

Norsk militærpoliti får «undervisning»:
– KGB står bak same-aksjonene

Av Frank Helgesen

●— Det er Sovjetunionen som står bak den stigende nasjonalfølelsen hos samene. KGB står bak en rekke slike undergravingsforsøk i den vestlige verden der de setter minoritetsgrupper opp mot det nasjonale samfunnet. De støtter disse gruppene for å skade de pro-vestlige nasjonene. Kravet om et eget sameland i Norden er resulatet av slik undergraving fra KGB's side.»

Det er major Tore Storebakken som hevder dette i et undervisningshefte om KGB's metoder. Dette heftet brukes i opplæring av militærpolitiet i Norge. Trykksaken hans heter «Forelesningshefte i sikkerhetstjeneste» med hovedtittel «Trusselen».

Ukeavisa «Dag og Tid» publiserer denne uke deler av heftet. Majoren tar der Nord-Norge med som et av de brennpunkt i verden der Sovjet forsøker å øke sin innflytelse. Strategene i Kreml benytter seg av samene i dette spillet, hevder han.

Sitat fra undervisningsheftet:

«...te delmål er etablering ... nasjonal frigjerings-...e, blant samene. Når

denne bevegelsen får gjort nok oppstyr, vil Sovjet iverksette en «politiaksjon» for å beskytte en undertrykt minoritet. Dette arbeidet er ivaretatt gjennom et intensivt undergravingsarbeid. Det er dannet en frigjøringsbevegelse blant samene. De vil reise krav om et område som omfatter Norge sørover til Snåsa, Nordkalottområdene i Sverige og Finland, samt for syns skyld Kola-halvøya.

Forfatteren er skremt over utviklingen, skriver han i sitt hefte. Han hevder at norske myndigheter har pålagt seg selv for store restriksjoner når det gjelder militær aktivitet i nord, samt at forsvarets beredskapsevne er sterkt svekket og «av velferdsmessig karakter».

Kort og godt den gamle visa om at soldatene har det for godt og at forsvaret derfor er svekket.

Når det gjelder bevisstgjøringen av samefolket, ser majoren ikke andre grunner til at dette har kommet i stand enn at KGB har fått i stand uroen. Den voksende nasjonalfølelsen er et klart uttrykk for at KGB er i sving i Nord-Norge. Utviklingen viser at deres arbeidsmønster avtegner seg nok en gang. Dette arbeidsmønstret følger følgende punkter ifølge undervisningsheftet:

Opprette og støtte frigjøringsbevegelse. Deretter opprette og støtte terrorgrupper fra denne bevegelsen. Ødelegge næringslivet gjennom forskjellige tiltak (de lave prisene

på Lada-bilder nevnes spesielt i heftet). Så følger: Skape eller utnytte motsetningsforhold på grunnlag av språk, religion eller etniske grupperinger. Infiltrere i kulturelle, religiøse og politiske organisasjoner.

Det er vel liten tvil om at majorens «undervisning» vil skape sterke motreaksjoner hos representanter for norske samer. At det arbeidet de har utført for å fremme samefolkets interesser blir karakterisert som et resultat av KGB's undergravningspolitikk og støtte, vil neppe falle i god jord.

Majorens beviser for sin teori må utstå i dagens avis da han for tida ikke er tilgjengelig for kommentar.

The Norwegian daily *Dagbladet* suspects the KGB of orchestrating Sámi resistance, April 18, 1980.

Sámi are parasites who get unreasonable subsidies, such as snowmobiles and bank loans with special conditions, while lying about the number of reindeer killed in order to claim government compensation; there are the accusations of the Sámi being "antisocial," as they allegedly take from society without giving anything in return; there are the accusations of their organizations being infiltrated by communists or the KGB itself; there are the Sámi women with excellent qualifications who don't get jobs as domestic helpers because Norwegians don't want them to be near their children. . . .

I have seen young Norwegians being bullied at work when it became known that they were dating a Sámi. I have also witnessed—luckily, to a lesser degree—even more harmful expressions of anti-Sámi hatred, for example when a young woman was driven from a Norwegianized community, or when I had patients come see me after having been attacked and severely injured by groups of young men for no other reason than wearing traditional Sámi clothing.[37]

33

Cultural exploitation

In 1991, Nils-Aslak Valkeapää received the Nordic Council Literature Prize for his poetry collection *Beaivi, áhčážan* (published in English as *The Sun, My Father*). When he stepped on stage for his acceptance speech, he pointed out that while all of the national flags of the Nordic countries were present, the Sámi flag was not. He called this "shameful" and hoisted a flag he had brought himself on the microphone stand.

Things have improved since then and more attention is being paid to the symbolic and cultural integration of the Sámi. Valkeapää himself took part in the opening ceremony of the Winter Olympics in Lillehammer, Norway, in 1994.

But cultural inclusion can also mean cultural exploitation, not least in the context of the tourist industry. Opinions also differ with respect to the public use of Sámi art; not all Sámi were happy when parts of the Akkats hydroelectric power station near Jåhkåmåhke were covered with Sámi motifs. Even in seemingly progressive projects, cultural inclusion can take on dubious forms; one example is the Norwegian animated film *Free Jimmy* (2006), which, next to vegan straight edge activists and an elephant on drugs, features a ruthless Sámi biker gang.

It is easy to feel provoked by symbolic gestures—or to regard them as mere tokens—when they are not met with improvements on the ground. The perhaps most striking example is that both Sweden and Finland, who fancy themselves forerunners of human rights in the global arena, have yet to ratify the ILO Convention 169. The main reason they haven't is that, in both countries, it is still the government that owns all the land in the parts of Sápmi they govern. Article 14 of ILO 169 states clearly: "The rights of ownership and possession of the peoples concerned over the lands which they traditionally occupy shall be recognised."[38] It's a legal dilemma the governments want to dodge.[39]

"Green colonialism"

For many years, Sámi activists and environmentalists found common cause in their opposition to mining, clear-cuts, and hydroelectric power stations. In recent years, however, this union of interests has been challenged, as Sápmi has become a popular site for wind farms. While wind power is hailed as a renewable and sustainable energy source, wind farms make huge areas of land unsuitable for reindeer herding, as reindeer take long detours to avoid the humming, awkward-looking turbines on their grazing grounds. Some environmentalists also object to motorized reindeer herding, and animal rights activists have voiced concern over both the treatment of the reindeer and—perhaps somewhat ironically—the hunting of predators such as wolves, lynx, and bears, which the Sámi find necessary to protect their herds. About fifty thousand reindeer are killed by predators every year; one lynx alone can kill one hundred in a season.[40]

Militarism

There is a strong military presence in Sápmi. When I did research for this book in Jåhkåmåhke in May 2019, with the tourist season still a month away, I had pitched the only tent at the local campground. All of the cabins were occupied, however—by US military personnel. And when eating lunch in town, I regularly sat next to a platoon of Swedish soldiers.

The situation in Norway appears to be similar, as described in a *Guardian* article from 2016: "The Oskal family have spent years resisting plans by the Norwegian army to expand the Mauken-Blafjell military area for anti-terrorism training. They lost one case, with the result that there are now roads and huts dotted across their pastures. Daniel Oskal's reindeer are now the only ones in the world accustomed to machine-gun fire."[41]

While the military presence of both occupying and foreign powers might not be among the Sámi's biggest concerns, it is a clear violation of their sovereignty, not least considering the complete absence of organized fighting forces in the people's history.

Litigation

Time and time again, Sámi find themselves in legal twists with landowners and the colonial governments. Some of the laws pertaining to Sámi access to traditional pastures and fishing and hunting grounds as well as to border crossings date back several hundred years. This makes them the subject of regular interpretative disagreement. Take the example of the Saarivuoma sameby: based in Sweden, the Norwegian government grants members the century-old right to lead their reindeer to summer pastures on Norwegian territory; however, it has also declared the permanent structures they have built there to be illegal, as they don't comply with "traditional use." In simple terms, to comply with the law, the Sámi are expected to bring tents. Legal cases such as this one—sometimes of Kafkaesque dimensions—draw energy and resources and distract from more basic questions about self-rule and autonomy.

The Rise of the Far Right

The rise of the Far Right in recent years has not bypassed the Nordic countries. This has put additional pressure on the Sámi. With the Norwegian Progress Party, the Sweden Democrats, and the True Finns, there are now far-right parties in the parliaments of all Nordic countries. Russian politics are also haunted by the specter of national chauvinism.

The far-right approach to the Sámi is reminiscent of the "lapp shall be lapp" policies of old. As advocates of national unity and identity, right-wingers often express sympathy for the Sámi's right to their language and culture. Yet they want to keep that language and culture completely separate from majority culture. Norwegian, Swedish, and Finnish law should in no way be compromised by special rights for minorities or people who are not considered to belong to the Norwegian, Swedish, or Finnish nation. While the Progress Party in Norway wants to abolish the Sámi Parliament, the Sweden Democrats want to do away with the Sámi's exclusive right to reindeer herding.

Hateful far-right propaganda against the Sámi is rare, although it does occur. In Finnmark, "white power" flyers appeared on the eve of the implementation of the Finnmark Act. But such blatant expressions of anti-Sámi sentiment are not required to understand that the Far Right is a threat. Prominent Sámi artists such as Maxida Märak and Sofia Jannok regularly support antifascist causes.

Current Sámi Activism

Maxida Märak and Sofia Jannok belong to a new generation of Sámi artists who are unabashedly political. They are joined by people such as singer Ella Marie Hætta Isaksen, film and theater director Pauliina Feodoroff, and visual artists Anders Sunna, Máret Ánne Sara, and the Suohpanterror collective. However, it is difficult,

Sámi resistance/ČSV patch (origins unclear).

if not impossible, to distinguish "political" from "nonpolitical" artists in Sápmi. Arts and politics are so closely intertwined that "artivism" has become a bon mot among scholars and journalists. There are political connotations in the work of the visual artists united in the Dáiddadállu collective of Guovdageaidnu, in the film and television work of Suvi West and Anne-Kirste Aikio, and in a thriving Sámi rap scene that includes acts such as Duolva Duottar, SlinCraze, Áilu Valle, and Amoc, who raps in Aanaar Sámi, spoken by less than four hundred people.

Like their forerunners, contemporary Sámi activists draw inspiration both from indigenous peoples and other minorities fighting for their rights. Sámi artist Carola Grahn has introduced the term "Sámi rage" in reference to the 1968 book *Black Rage*, authored by African American psychiatrists William H. Grier and Price M. Cobbs. Grahn explains, "What is interesting about using the book is to understand mental health problems and rage as a consequence of oppression, and to see how this applies to the mental health situation among Sámi."[42]

Culture remains an important element in the Sámi's relationship to other indigenous peoples. The Riddu Riđđu Festival for indigenous music and art near Romsa, organized since 1991, brings international guests to Sápmi every year. There is also increased international networking among scholars, for example in the Native American and Indigenous Studies Association.

Sámi are also represented in international social justice campaigns. There were strong Sámi contingents in the indigenous blocs marching at the time of the 2015 Climate Change Conference in Paris, and several Sámi delegations traveled to the Standing Rock Indian Reservation in 2016 to join the Dakota Pipeline protests.

In Sápmi, protests of recent years addressed a variety of concerns, reaching from mining plans at Raavrhjohke, in the south of Sápmi, to a massive Arctic railway project conceived on the Finnish side. Máret Ánne Sara's efforts in supporting her brother Jovsset Ánte, whom the Norwegian government has ordered to cull so many reindeer that reindeer herding could no longer provide a viable income for him, has drawn much public attention. After having lost his case in the Supreme Court of Norway, Jovsset Ánte Sara has now taken it to the UN Human Rights Committee. At the time of writing, it was still pending.

Resistance against new fishing regulations along the Deatnu River, which constitutes the border between Norway and Finland along a 252 km stretch, received significant media attention. The new legislation affects in particular Sámi who have been net fishing salmon in the river for centuries. When it was passed in 2017, Sámi activists erected a camp on the river island of Čearretsuolu and announced a moratorium. They returned to the island in the summers of 2018 and 2019. While the governments of Norway and Finland have not revoked legislation, they have not interfered with the moratorium either.

The most publicized Sámi protest movement of recent years was the one against the mining plans in Gállok, outside of Jåhkåmåhke.

In 2006, the UK-registered company Beowulf Mining received a ten-year permit to test drill for iron ore in Gállok, which lies within the lands used by the sameby of Jåhkågasska tjielldes. Similar to developments in Áltá, a protest movement emerged that brought together a broad coalition of Sámi, environmentalists, and social justice advocates. The movement gained particular

"Resistance is growing." Protest camp in Gállok, 2013 (kolonierna.wordpress. com).

momentum after Beowulf chairman Clive Sinclair-Poulton declared at a 2013 stakeholder meeting in Stockholm that his standard response to people in the UK inquiring about the "locals' opinion" was to show them a picture of the forests of northern Sweden, asking, "What local people?" "Us Local People" became the rallying cry of several campaigns started in response.

A protest camp was erected in Gállok in 2013 on the access road to the drilling site. It remained impassable for vehicles for several weeks, despite repeated police attempts to clear it. Workshops, lectures, and performances were organized, and a delegation of the Sámi Parliament came to visit. On September 3, 2013, bulldozers arrived and cleared a new path through the forest, bypassing the barricades. The day after, the camp was abandoned. The protests, however, continued.

At the 2014 Jåhkåmåhke Winter Market, an event that attracts thousands of tourists every year, an activist group including Maxida Märak organized a "black reindeer caravan" to emphasize that continued mining would eventually lead to the death of reindeer herding. (A regular reindeer caravan—*ráidu* in Sámi—is one of the highlights of the market every year.) In black clothing, with their faces painted white, the activists led their reindeer in a silent procession. The image was striking.

The action provoked much hostility from locals in favor of mining, but this did not deter the group from staging another protest at the market the following year. They stopped the Swedish minister for culture, Alice Bah Kuhnke, on the way to her hotel to read the "Sámi Manifesto 15" (see pages 169–70) while Maxida Märak cut off her sibling Timimie's hair.

At the time of writing, the future of mining in Gállok is unclear. Both the Sámi Parliament and county authorities have objected to the project, but the Swedish government has not yet decided how to proceed.

On the Road to Self-Determination

In his 1971 book *Greetings from Lappland: The Sami—Europe's Forgotten People*, Nils-Aslak Valkeapää wrote: "The Samis do not aim for their own state. That would be too unrealistic." Harald Gaski confirmed this in his introduction to the 1994 anthology *Sami Culture in a New Era*:

> Sami policy has never been directed toward the establishment of a separate Sami nation-state. Instead, it has concentrated more on establishing rights that will assure the survival and growth of the Sami and their culture in their own ancestral areas of settlement. Even during periods of the most aggressive colonization and assimilation, as well as during the Christianization by force that took place in the eighteenth and nineteenth centuries, the Sami turned to their own cultural expressions as an internal defense against external pressure.[43]

The Sámi are a minority almost everywhere they live, and the establishment of a Sámi state seems like a logistical impossibility that would entail high economic risks.[44] It is also an alien concept to a people who come from a stateless tradition.

This, of course, requires concepts that can bring the notion of self-determination—which is frequently invoked by Sámi activists—to fulfillment without having one's own state. What exactly does self-determination mean under such circumstances? It is a difficult question, but not without precedents. The Zapatistas have been very clear in their demands for autonomy without evoking the goal of a separate state. The Kurdish movement has abandoned the goal for a Kurdish state in favor of what has become known as "democratic confederalism." Nunavut is a Canadian territory largely under indigenous administration. Closer to Sápmi, the islands of Åland, part of the Finnish state but Swedish-speaking, form an autonomous region. The Swedish speakers on the Finnish mainland, about 5 percent of the overall population, have far-reaching minority rights to protect their language and culture. And in Sápmi itself, the world natural heritage site of Laponia is referred to on Wikipedia as "the world's largest unmodified nature area to be still cultured by natives."[45] Then there are the Sámi parliaments, a significant political infrastructure already in place, even if their powers may still be limited. But what if those powers were to be extended? These, and many other matters, will be discussed in the following interviews.

NOTES

1   United Nations Human Rights Council, *Report of the Special Rapporteur* . . . , 4.
2   "Samerna i siffor," www.samer.se/samernaisiffror.
3   In Norway and Sweden, reindeer herding is the exclusive right of the Sámi. Regulations are looser in Finland, and altogether different in Russia, where reindeer herding is practiced by different peoples in the Arctic region.
4   There are also cultural divides that cause some observers to single out particular Sámi groups as clearly distinct from others. This applies, for example, to the Aanaar Sámi, which are exclusively found in a relatively small area around the town of Aanaar, and the Skolt Sámi who, among other characteristic features, are adherents of the Christian Orthodox faith. To explore these differences further lies beyond the scope of this book.
5   In 2018, the Stockholm-based Sámi sisters Johanna and Maria Tjäder launched a podcast entitled "Asphalt Sámi" (*Asfaltssamer*).
6   Harald Gaski, "The Sami People: The 'White Indians' of Scandinavia," *American Indian Culture and Research Journal*, 17, no. 1 (1993), 116.
7   Christian Mériot, *Samerna* (Furulund: Alhambra, 1994), 4.
8   *Let the River Flow: The Sovereign Will and the Making of a New Worldliness*, exhibition catalog, 2018, 10.
9   Quoted from *Samernas tid, del 2: Gränser genom Sápmi*, documentary film (2017).
10 Victoria Harnesk, "You Have to Be Visible—to Exist?," open letter to Swedish Prime Minister Göran Persson and UN Secretary General Kofi Annan regarding the Stockholm International Forum Conference on the Holocaust, January 25, 2004. Quoted from www.klevius.info/genocide-1.pdf. Edited for clarity by G.K.

11 "Voices from a Teachers' Room in the Municipality of Vyöddale," in Helena Carlsson, *Same och lapp i tid och ord* (Skellefteå: Ord och visor, 2006), 13. Translated by G.K.

12 *Let the River Flow*, 16.

13 In 1937, when reindeer herding had become established in Alaska, the authorities prohibited non-Alaskans, including Sámi, from owning reindeer. Some of the Sámi reindeer herders returned to the Nordic countries, others moved to the contiguous United States.

14 "Sami History," Sami Cultural Center of North America, http://www.samiculturalcenter.org/sami-history-and-culture/sami-history/.

15 A Pacific Sámi Searvi in Washington State is no coincidence. In the 1930s, a Sámi fellowship was founded on the Kitsap Peninsula near Seattle. Many of the Sámi reindeer herders working in Alaska who decided not to return to Europe after they had lost their right to owning reindeer in 1937, made their way to Washington State. The Sámi Cultural Center of North America sponsors a traveling exhibition, *Sami Reindeer People of Alaska*, which has been shown in fifteen towns across North America as well as in Jåhkåmåhke.

16 The official explanations for the practice cited both medical and social reasons. The law, in fact, did not condone forced sterilization, but later government investigations came to the conclusion that about half of the sixty-three thousand people sterilized from 1934 to 1975 were not consulted. People undergoing sex change were forcibly sterilized until 2012.

17 "Samers hälsa," Region Norbotten website, September 25, 2018, http://www.norrbotten.se/sv/Utveckling-och-tillvaxt/Folkhalsa/Fokusomraden/Samers-halsa/.

18 Elsa Laula, *Inför lif eller död* (Stockholm: Wilhelmssons, 1904), 27–29. Translated by G.K.

19 Sámi skiing expertise was also cherished in Arctic expeditions. In 1883, Pava Lars Nilsson Tuorda and Anders Rassa rose to international fame when they covered a distance of 285 miles in 57 hours during a reconnaissance trip of Greenland.

20 The English spelling traditionally used is "Saami Council." Here, it has been adapted to the spellings used in this book.

21 Quoted from Sametinget, *Sametinget—10 år* (Kiruna, 2003), n.p.

22 *Let the River Flow*, 5.

23 Josefina Skerk, "SD vill rensa bort samernas kultur," *Aftonbladet*, August 26, 2018, www.aftonbladet.se/ledare/a/zLjql1/sd-vill-rensa-bort-samernas-kultur.

24 Harald Gaski, "Introduction," *Sami Culture in a New Era* (Kárášjohka: Davvi Girji, 1997), 21.

25 That number is disputed. One of the participants told me, "There were certainly more—but everyone says it was seven, so let it be seven." I follow that advice.

26 Björn Forseth, *Samelands historia* (Solna: Ekelunds förlag, 2000), 270.

27 Samiskt informationscentrum, *Samerna: Ett av världens urfolk* (n.p., n.d.), 22. Translated by G.K.

28 Per Otnes, "Nykolonialisme i Sameland," in Lina R. Homme, ed., *Nordisk nykolonialisme* (Oslo: Samlaget, 1969), 52.

29 These are references to Dee Brown's book *Bury My Heart at Wounded Knee* (1970), and to Pile o' Bones, once the name of today's Regina, Saskatchewan, named after the huge piles of buffalo bones erected by Cree living in the area.

30 Ande Somby, "Charta 79," interview, April 2018, leaflet by the Nomadic Library.

31 There was a follow-up to the festival in 1993.

32 Gaski, "Introduction," 17.

33 Göran Lundin, *Samerna i Sverige* (Stockholm: Oktoberförlaget, 1977), 11–12.

34 Quoted from Nina Berglund, "Parliament to Study Sami, Kven History," June 13, 2007, www.newsinenglish.no.

35 I am not going to address analytical questions about whether anti-Sámi prejudices constitute a form of racism or not, as such discussions lie beyond the scope of this book. The term is commonly used by Sámi themselves.

36 The report, *Kartläggning av rasism mot samer i Sverige* (A Survey of Racism against Sámi in Sweden), has been criticized for lack of scientific scrutiny, yet the data it collects does reflect widespread perceptions among Sámi living in Sweden.

37 Per Fugelli, "Rasisme i Finnmark," in *Samisk mot—norsk hovmod*, ed. Gunnar H. Gjenset (Oslo: Pax, 1981), 84–85.

38 Quoted from www.ilo.org/ilolex/cgi-lex/convde.pl?C169.

39 About the implementation of ILO 169 in Norway, see the interview with Øyvind Ravna in this book. Russia has not ratified the convention either.

40 John Vidal, "Sami Reindeer Herders Battle Conservationists and Miners to Cling On to Arctic Culture," *Guardian*, February 21, 2016, www.theguardian.com/global-development/2016/feb/21/sami-people-reindeer-herders-arctic-culture.

41 Vidal, "Sami Reindeer Herders Battle Conservationists and Miners."

42 Carola Grahn and Sigbjørn Skåden, "Hjärnkontor," *Hjärnstorm*, no. 128 (*Samisk vrede*), 2017, n.p.

43 Gaski, "Introduction," 9.

44 An independent Sámi state—and its possible consequences and conflicts—are the topic of the 2013 theater play *ČSV-republihkka* by Siri Broch Johansen.

45 Nine samebyar using the area for reindeer herding are involved in administering the site. See Carina Green, *Managing Laponia: A World Heritage Site as Arena for Sami Ethno-Politics in Sweden* (Uppsala: Acta Universitatis Upsaliensis, 2009).

Hans Ragnar Mathisen, "It Is Happening . . ." 1981 (BONO/Artists Rights Society, New York). Hans Ragnar Mathisen, a.k.a. Keviselie (born 1945), is a prolific Sámi artist, well known for his maps of Sápmi. Visit www.keviselie-hansragnarmathisen.net for more information about his life and work.

INTERVIEWS

Synnøve Persen

Photo: Susanne Hætta

Synnøve Persen (born 1950) is a visual artist and poet who has been a pivotal figure in Norwegian cultural politics and the organization of Sámi artists. She was a member of the influential Máze Group, an active participant in the resistance against the Áltá-Guovdageaidnu dam project, and one of the hunger strikers of 1979. Synnøve has received numerous awards from Sámi and Norwegian institutions. For more information about her work, see www.synnovepersen.no. We sat down for a talk at her home in Porsáŋgu in June 2019.

It is often said that the so-called Áltá controversy instigated a new Sámi resistance movement. Is that true?

Yes, I would say that's true. The week of the hunger strike in 1979 was one of the weeks when everything changes. Most importantly, it began to dawn on the people of Norway what was actually happening in Sápmi. They didn't know, and the authorities didn't want them to know. Many Norwegians hardly knew that Sámi existed outside of museums; they had no concept of us as living people. This was a week of revelation.

The protests in Áltá gathered people from around the country. The fight for Sámi rights was part of it, but the movement was bigger than that. Environmentalists, farmers, salmon fishers— many were involved. That's what made it so special. There was a strong sense of solidarity.

The 1970s were a very different time from now. There were social movements around the world, which, of course, influenced us, too. I have said many times that I belong to the first generation of Sámi who received higher education: we got to finish primary school, move on to high school, and many of us ended up at universities. There, we got caught up in the student culture of the 1970s. We felt we belonged to a new community.

Many university students and professors were involved in the Áltá conflict. Professors came to the protest camp, which created much media attention. Everyone had to cover what was happening in Áltá. The media played a very important role in those days. This was a long time before Facebook!

Was the coverage mainly critical or sympathetic?

There were, of course, some critical voices, but most of it was sympathetic. The critical voices got drowned out quickly.

Can you tell us about the hunger strike in 1979?

We had a meeting with the prime minister. Our most important demands were a stop of the construction along the river and an investigation into Sámi rights. We gave the government a deadline—I think it was noon the next day—and said that we'd go on hunger strike if the demands weren't met. I don't think anyone thought that we'd actually do it. But we did.

How did you get involved in it?
I don't exactly know, to be honest. Many things just happened at that time. I remember someone coming to Máze to discuss the idea with us. Then some people drove to Oslo through Sweden. I wasn't able to come along, but I took a plane to Oslo a couple of days later. We had the meeting with the prime minister, and then things developed as they did. We weren't really prepared for it. We had no experience with hunger strikes, and not in our wildest dreams did we expect so much support in Oslo. Everything happened right outside the parliament building. It was a very intense week.

There was another hunger strike two years later. Were the same people involved?
Some people were the same. The hunger strike in 1981 lasted much longer. People were harmed for life. I was asked to join but said no.

Why?
I had become a mother. It would have not only affected me but my daughter as well. I was also asked to join the group of women who ended up occupying the prime minister's office. I had said yes at first but decided not to join them at the very last minute, after a sleepless night. I wanted to stay with my daughter.

It seems somewhat ironic that the Áltá protests are usually described as a success, when the power plant was still built.
The protests changed the country, and that was the most important thing. They made the people of Norway aware of a situation they knew nothing about before. And we had gotten so much support that it was impossible for the authorities not to react. The Norwegian government's attitude toward the Sámi clearly changed after that.

How did the Máze Group fit into this?
Perfectly!

But its foundation was independent of the Áltá conflict...
It had nothing to do with it. We were young Sámi artists who had finished our education, and we wanted to return to Sápmi and

found an arts collective. That was in 1978. A year later, the Álta conflict came to a head. Máze played an important role, because according to the original plans for the dam from the early 1970s, the entire community would have been flooded. So, when we arrived, people were very conscious of the government's plans. When the protests started in 1979, it was natural that we would be a part of them. Our house became a base for protesters. There were always people sleeping on the floor and so on. We weren't able to do any art, but it was an exciting time.

How did this affect you as an arts collective? Would the artistic development of the group have been different had none of this happened?
That's hard to say. You can always talk about ifs and whens, but what's the point? You can't live several lives at once. We happened to be there at the time of the Álta conflict. That's our history.

The Máze Group dissolved in 1983. Why?
We were always struggling economically. What we did was an entirely new thing for Finnmark. We were dependent on funds, but no group like us had ever asked for funding. Before we came, there were maybe three professional artists in the whole county, and now seven of us arrived at once. We were a long way from anywhere. There was no market for art, and no infrastructure. The odds were stacked against us, but we felt strong as a group. However, when an application for financial support from Norway's Regional Development Fund was rejected in 1983, we gave up. Little did we know at the time how much influence our efforts would have on the development of Sámi art in general. That only became obvious years later.

You've been very involved in the development of Sámi art, cofounding several organizations for Sámi artists. Would this have been such a significant part of your biography without the Máze Group?
In one way or another, I would have gotten involved in cultural politics regardless. To strengthen the position of Sámi artists has always been very important to me. In 1974, my uncle, the composer John Persen, led protests by artists in Norway demanding better working conditions. This inspired me very much.

You are known both as a painter and a poet. Sámi artists often express themselves in various ways. How do you explain this?
To have more than one leg to stand on has always been part of our culture. Specialization was a luxury we couldn't afford. If you're up in the mountains in the middle of winter and all you know is math, you will die. You need to be able to fix things. There is no one else to do it. All of my uncles were fantastic handymen, able to fix anything. The basis of Sámi culture is survival, and in order to survive you need to do many things.

It also seems near impossible to separate art from politics in Sápmi.
Traditionally, there was no word for art in the Sámi language. There was *duodji* for handicraft, and *dáidu* for knowledge. Today, the word *dáidda* is used for art, but it was only introduced with the Máze Group. This proves how closely art is tied into Sámi life. When a new word enters a language, it tells you that something important is happening.

In recent years, a new generation of Sámi artists including Anders Sunna, Máret Ánne Sara, and the Suohpanterror collective has received much attention. The political element in their art is very obvious. In yours, it is not. Does that mean that your art is less political, or is it political in a different way?
I decided very early on that I was not going to do propagandist art. I am a modernist, and I find the language of abstract painting very strong. I have been asked many times why I wasn't a "political artist," and my usual response is that I am a Sámi artist. Being a Sámi artist is very political; you don't need to propagate anything.

But there is no problem with Sámi artists who do?
No, that's fantastic! When we talk about Anders Sunna and Máret Ánne Sara, for example, it has so much to do with their lives and their families as well.

Please tell us about the Sámi flag.
When I was a student at the National Academy of Fine Arts in Oslo, we went on a trip to the Faroe Islands in 1977. Faroe artists were very interested in Sámi artists, because the Faroe Islands were also

colonized, by Denmark. That part was great. What was not so great was that I got so seasick on the way there that I couldn't imagine returning by boat.

As I was sitting on the flight from Tórshavn to Copenhagen, looking at the Scandinavian landmass underneath, I realized that my country had no colors. A flag appeared in my mind and, upon my return, I sat down to sew a prototype: red, yellow, and blue in vertical stripes, very similar to the flag that was made Sápmi's official flag by the Sámi Council in 1986. It was important to me not to have a cross in it. All Scandinavian flags do.

The prototype is now in Norway's National Museum. For twenty-five years, I had no idea where it was. But then someone brought it back to me, and the museum bought it in 2017.

When the Sámi Council asked for proposals for a Sámi flag in 1986, you didn't send in yours. Why?

I felt I had done my part. The flag was widely used during the Álta conflict. It had caused more controversy than I ever imagined.

In what way?

I think it was seen as provoking conflict. As if I was advocating a separate Sámi state, with a possible civil war as a consequence. Even relatives thought I had gone too far. World War II had had a terrible impact on Finnmark, and people were very afraid of that. For me, these fears were far-fetched and I was caught completely by surprise. But then things changed with the Álta conflict, and the flag turned into a symbol of Sámi pride. It always flew at the protest camp and sent a clear message to the police: "This is our land. It is not Norway."

You described the movement against the Álta dam as a broad solidarity movement that the Sámi were part of. Is there much solidarity with Sámi struggles today?

In certain contexts, yes. For example, with regard to wind power, which has become a big issue. I'm not as involved today as I was during the Álta conflict, but the Sámi aren't alone in fighting the construction of wind farms in reindeer-herding areas and islands along the coast. Many people are concerned about the impact on local wildlife and on natural diversity, all of which is threatened by artificial elements like wind turbines being planted in the landscape. These are positive developments.

What else gives you hope?

Porsáŋgu, which is my home, was always multicultural. There are Sámi, Kven, and Norwegians. We all have our own languages, and today this is officially recognized. It is important to acknowledge that our society is not one-dimensional, because the world is not one-dimensional. We meet more and more different cultures in our immediate environment because of migration caused by poverty and war. For us, meeting other cultures is nothing unusual; we have done it for hundreds of years. We also know what it's like to be oppressed, discriminated against, and made invisible—and not by strangers, but by your own neighbors. It is no coincidence that many refugees have found new homes in Finnmark.

The Sámi Parliament is also important with regard to multiculturalism. It is true that is has no political power, but it is not a purely symbolic institution either. It maintains close relations to indigenous peoples around the world, which is very important for us: we share similar histories, and it is crucial for us to hear their stories and how they've been able to resist and persevere.

One must not be afraid all the time. Despite everything we've experienced, we are still here, and we will continue to be here. When I was a child, I never thought I'd be part of something historic. There are always important things to fight for. You might not always achieve your goals, but when you make an effort, there is little more that can be asked of you.

The Land Outside the Map

Synnøve Persen

Presented at the Thinking at the Edge of the World conference in Longyearbyen/Svalbard, Norway, June 12, 2016.

When Ottar the earl of Håløyg sailed north along the cost of Finnmark to the Kola Peninsula in the ninth century, he reported to the King of England he saw no one else than some Sami until he rounded the peninsula by the White Sea. So what happened to this land? How did it disappear? Where did it go?

I live in the land of devils, witches, monsters, they've said, in the land outside the map, in the nothingness, in a history beyond history. The Sami history made invisible. On the "real" map the Sami names are washed out, do not exist. Every mountain, every lake, the remotest places.

Where is my land? Is it a trauma? A dream? A Utopia?

Who are we? Strangers? Foreigners? Guests in our own land? Brainwashed to believe the pseudo-stories about ourselves.

A history the modern Scandinavian states do not want to hear about themselves. No, there were no military forces, no shooting, no killing, they did it in a human way. Their refined cruelty. The assimilation programs. Loss of language, culture, history, land. The shame brought upon us.

Ottar the earl sails on. The land is explored, the people civilized and tamed to silence. This time to suck the rest of the fjords, the mountains, the fish in the big ocean. All the resources, the natural richness of the Arctic.

She is an extremist. Do not listen to her, we've been supervising her a while.

The voice of the poet. The need for a voice.

We have given this people citizenship, equality, welfare, education. What do they want? Back to the stone age? We want stability in the region. Borders. Control. We've saved this uncivilized people from poverty, taught them to read and write our language. The poets should tell stories of beauty, the northern light, the midnight sun.

We have no problems. We have solved them by eating them. We own the land. You are our citizens.

Unsubscribe the map of the colonizers.

Niillas Somby

Photo courtesy of Niillas Somby

Niillas Somby (born 1948) has been a prominent figure in the Sámi's struggle for justice since the 1970s. He was severely injured in an ill-fated 1982 sabotage action and subsequently found refuge among First Nations in British Columbia. He has worked as a reindeer herder, sailor, mechanic, photographer, and journalist. Today, he lives in Deanušaldi, where I met him in June 2019.

The documentary film *Give Us Our Skeletons* follows your successful quest to have the Norwegian authorities release the skull of your ancestor Mons Aslaksen Somby, who was executed as a leader in the so-called Guovdageaidnu Rebellion. Can you shed some light on the family connection?

My family originally comes from the region of Guovdageaidnu. Let me start with an anecdote . . .

My great-grandfather, Nils Johnsen Somby, had the summer pastures for his reindeer up at the North Cape. He had many reindeer and was a rich man. There was a local community in the area that was under total control of a trader who owned a grocery store and bought the local fishers' catch. One year, when there was a very bad fishing season, he packed up and moved on. The local fishers were left with nothing. My great-grandfather bought all of the properties in the community and allowed them to stay there. He never told anyone, as this was a very unusual thing for Sámi to do.

Decades later, in the 1970s, my father received a letter from the National Association of Reindeer-Herding Sámi in Norway. They asked about one Nils Johnsen Somby, who by then had passed away. My father had inherited the community.

It was very isolated and by then completely abandoned, and we had no idea where it was. The consequences of the Guovdageaidnu Rebellion and the border regulations between Norway, Sweden, and Finland had caused my family to move farther east. I joined my father in finding the place. It was difficult, we had no maps or anything else to rely on. Once we found it, we were stunned by how beautiful it was. There wasn't much left of the buildings, only a few stones. But there was plenty of plastic along the beach: dishwashing gloves, toothbrushes, dildos—it was rather absurd. For the first time, I became aware of the enormous problems caused by the plastic in our oceans.

Anyway, this is just to illustrate that you inherit many problems, and with them the responsibility to fix them. The same was true for the skull of my relative taken by the Norwegian authorities.

How did you eventually retrieve it?

It took many years of dealing with colonial bureaucracy. In 1997, 143 years after they had been executed, Mons Aslaksen Somby and Aslak Jacobsen Hætta finally got a proper burial.

Can you give us your interpretation of the Guovdageaidnu Rebellion?

Læstadianism is the usual explanation. But you first have to explain Læstadianism.

Læstadianism could take hold because Sámi society was in disarray. Colonialism had destroyed its values, and people drowned their sorrows in alcohol. If someone takes away all rules, there is chaos, and people look for new rules. Læstadius provided them. It's good trying to help people out of a crisis, but the price that the Sámi paid was enormous. The old ways were no longer respected. Traditional spirituality was gone. There was a new god, and the promise of a heaven with angels who sing and play harp.

You can see the same pattern everywhere colonialism took hold: traditional spirituality was the first element of the culture to be attacked. You find churches all across the colonized world, not least on the reservations and missions indigenous people were confined to. And you can see them on our mountains, too.

Of course, legal discrimination is a big part of colonialism. But the oppression of spirituality is a huge factor, which is all too often forgotten. It saddens me that there are so many of my own people who don't realize this. The traditional ways in which we related to nature and the world around us, were all based in spirituality. This had very concrete implications. When you were fishing, you were supposed to be quiet. Not primarily because you'd scare away the fish, but in order to respect the powers that allowed you to be there. And if you caught a fish, you treated it with respect, too. You never boasted about your catch. You were aware of whether you were fishing upstream or downstream, and if you prepared the fish by the river to eat, you did it in a particular way to show your appreciation. There were many simple ceremonies, as I call them. Today, they are largely forgotten.

You played a central role during another rebellious period in Sámi history, the Áltá conflict. How did you experience that time?

There was great optimism. I hoped that people would wake up and get real about Sámi rights. At the same time, we had to deal with contradictions. We were forced to claim "our" land, when, in reality, no land is ours. The land doesn't belong to us. We belong to the land, and it is our responsibility to take care of it.

The driving group behind the Álta protests was Folkeaksjonen, "People's Action." How was it organized?

There was no formal leadership, but some members had more respect than others and were better organizers. Folkeaksjonen wasn't a Sámi organization, even if Sámi were involved. At first, the protests really were about the protection of the river, not Sámi rights. But some Sámi members, such as Tore Bongo, built important bridges to the Norwegian population. The most important bridge, however, was the youth in Oslo. We had strong support when we erected a *lávvu* outside of parliament and went on hunger strike.

Sometimes, the Sámi protest movement of the 1970s and '80s is seen as part of the left-wing protest movements of the time. Is this a fair characterization?

There was some support from the left, and inevitably it has an impact on you, especially when there is hardly any support from anywhere else. But the movement was not controlled by the Left. Sámi were in full control.

The late Mikkel Eira, a leading figure in the hunger strikes of both 1979 and 1981, later expressed regrets. Why?

Mikkel didn't regret taking action, but he was disappointed with the outcome. It was great that the Álta movement put Sámi rights on the political agenda. But it also established a new class of Sámi politicians who soon claimed control over how these rights were to be implemented. Sámi activism was integrated into the colonial system, and people like us were told to be quiet. This is what frustrated Mikkel.

But aren't the ratification of the ILO Convention 169, the Sámi Parliament, and the Finnmark Act steps forward?

There are advantages and disadvantages with everything. But how it all happened was determined by one group of people. They always raised the specter of increased tension, possibly even war. But let's be real: there was no chance that Sámi resistance would have escalated into a war. There were way too many friendships and family ties at stake. Finnmark is sparsely populated, but social relationships are tight.

Top left: cover of Norway's *Miljømagasinet* no. 1, 1980. Top right: international call to join the protests against the Áltá-Guovdageaidnu River dam (private collection). Bottom left: poster for a solidarity event in Oslo during the Áltá crisis (Alta Museum). Bottom right: patches from the Áltá protests (private collection)

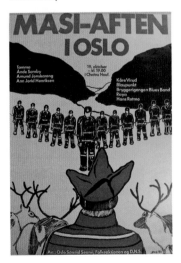

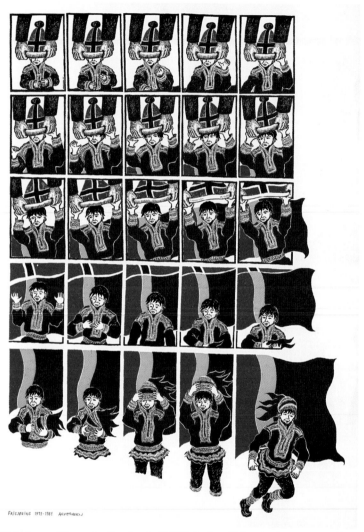

Arvid Sveen, "Emancipation," 1981 (BONO/Artists Rights Society, New York). Arvid Sveen is a Norwegian artist whose work was highly influential during the Sámi civil rights movement. The poster "Emancipation" emerged from the very first frame (top left), which Sveen drew for the Sámi newspaper *Ságat* in 1972. The theme was "Norwegian oppression." A decade later, Sámi liberation seemed on the horizon. The poster's final frames feature the original Sámi flag designed by Synnøve Persen.

Top: autobiographical accounts by John Reier Martinsen ("The Bridge") and Niillas Somby ("In the Hour of the Wolf"). Left: cover of *Charta 79* no. 6, 1980.

Top: Britta Marakatt-Labba, "The Crows," 1981 (BUS/Artists Rights Society, New York). This embroidered tapestry is one of the most famous depictions of the Álta protests. Britta Marakatt-Labba (born 1951) was a cofounder of the Máze Group. Bottom: Tomas Colbengtson, "Looking unto Jesus," screenprint on glass, 2015 (BUS/Artists Rights Society, New York). Tomas Colbengtson (born 1957) is a prolific South Sámi artist and writer. For more of his work visit www.colbengtson.com.

BRITTA MARAKATT - 1980

Left: Katarina Pirak Sikku, photograph from the exhibition *Nammaláhpán* (Nameless), 2014 (BUS/Artists Rights Society, New York). In her exhibition *Nammaláhpán*, Sámi artist Katarina Pirak Sikku (born 1965) explores the history of racial biology that the Sámi people were subjected to during the first half of the twentieth century. The exhibition is based on several years of research, including numerous interviews.

Art by Anders Sunna. Top: "Area Infected," 2014 (see pages 159–61); bottom: "Four Nation Army," 2013 (both BUS/Artists Rights Society, New York).

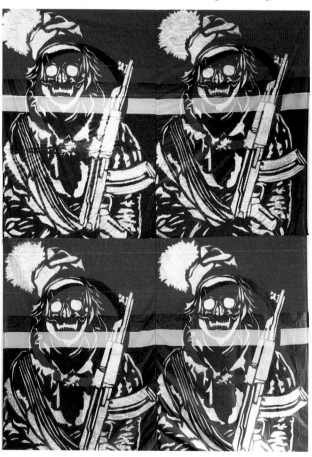

Art by Anders Sunna. Top: "Elsa Laula on Yellow Drum" (ca. 2014); bottom: iconic image created by Sunna, appearing all across Sápmi, here near Áltá, 2015 (both courtesy of Anders Sunna). For more of Sunna's art visit www.anderssunna.com.

Top: "black reindeer caravan" (*tjáhppis rájddo*) at the 2014 Jåhkåmåhke Winter Market (Anne-Marit Päiviö/Sveriges Radio Sameradion). Above: stage at the Gállok protest camp with a broad blend of signs and symbols: "Decolonized Zone," "Autonomous Norrland" ("Norrland" is a generic term for Sweden's northernmost provinces), "Refuse—Resist—Rewild," the Sámi flag, and a popular stencil by Anders Sunna (Gertrude Kuhmunen/Ája, Jåhkåmåhke). Right: sign at the Gállok protest camp (Ája, Jåhkåmåhke).

Top: Duodji Institute in Kárášjohka, bench in Jåhkåmåhke (both Gabriel Kuhn, 2019). Left: Sápmi Pride, Giron, 2014 (Sara Parkman/ www.saraparkman.tumblr. com). Bottom: photograph posted on Sámi artist Sofia Jannok's Facebook page in August 2016 under the heading "A message to North Dakota, US from Sápmi: We— rapper Amoc and me Sofia Jannok—stand with Standing Rock!" (photo: Paadar Images).

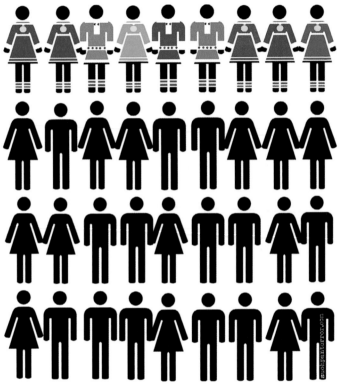

FRONTLINES OF CLIMATE CHANGE
FOREFRONT OF CHANGE
#EndCo2onialism

Suohpanterror, "EndCo2onialism," 2015 (www.suohpanterror.com).

Top: Máret Ánne Sara (center) and supporters protest outside the Parliament of Norway against the forced culling of reindeer imposed on Máret Ánne's brother Jovsset Ánte Sara, 2017 (Per Heimly). Bottom: Máret Ánne Sara, "The Norwegian Hunger Games," 2016 (BONO/Artists Rights Society, New York). See pages 91–92. For more information on how to support Jovsset Ánte Sara visit www.pileosapmi.com and www.wewhosupportjovssetante.org.

Images from the Deatnu River island of Čearretsuolu after a moratorium was declared regarding new fishing legislation for the Deatnu River in 2017 (courtesy of Ellos Deatnu/www.ellosdeatnu.wordpress.com).

When, in 1982, the Norwegian Supreme Court upheld the decision to build a power plant along the Álta-Guovdageaidnu River, you decided to engage in a sabotage action. A bridge leading to the construction site was supposed to be bombed. The action went tragically wrong. What happened?

It was a very cold night and we were three people on snowmobiles. When we had planted the bomb, one of my companions said that the battery had died. I went to change it. But as I pulled it out, the bomb went off. I was thrown through the air and landed in the snow. I was just lying there, and everything felt wonderful: the colors, the smell, the energy of the place. I thought, "Okay, I suppose this is what it's like to die. Maybe that's the meaning of life: to come to this perfect moment." Then I heard a companion, John Reier Martinsen, ask if I was still alive. I couldn't be bothered to respond, I was too content with where I was. I got irritated when he tied a scarf around my arm and lifted me up on his snowmobile. The perfect moment was gone. The world felt cold, dark, and ugly. John Reier took me to the hospital. I lost an eye and an arm, but my life was saved.

Apparently, the bomb could have done only minor damage. Was that intentional?

Yes. The action was meant to be symbolic. Everything about Álta was symbolic. It was street theater. In response to the Supreme Court's decision, we just wanted to use a different language.

When we went on hunger strike in 1979, we were naive enough to believe that the language of civil disobedience would suffice, that our demands would be met, and that the justice system was indeed just. We believed that if we went to the courts, they would make things right. We had no experience with the legal system at the time.

At the Álta protest camp, there was much yoiking and poetry. That language hadn't helped either. We wanted to try a different one, obviously without much success. The only thing I got out of that action is that there's now a bridge named after me.

Let us return to that night. You got to the hospital, you got treatment—and then you and John Reier were imprisoned.

At first, we were charged with arson, which carried a maximum sentence of twenty-one years. We were held in isolation at the prison in Romsa and treated like Norway's worst criminals—or "terrorists," as we were called.

And then you managed to escape to Canada.
That needed more street theater.

I contemplated my options. If I was really going to be sentenced to twenty-one years, I figured that I'd be an old man by the time I came out. My children would be adults. This was not going to work for me.

In isolation, you are not meant to get any outside information. But there are always ways to get some. I heard about two prisoners who had escaped and never been found. That came in handy.

I stopped eating. I didn't announce a hunger strike, I just stopped touching the food. With the help of a prison officer, I got one orange a day. I hoped that this would keep me going, until they sent me to the psychiatric ward, from where it would be easier to escape.

After one week, the warden came to see me. He was angry and asked me what the "hunger strike nonsense" was about. I told him that I wasn't on hunger strike, but that I didn't trust the food. I also told him that I considered no longer drinking the water as well. I wanted to make him understand that I was worried about being poisoned, even if I didn't say it out loud. The warden yelled, "Do you think we are murderers?"

"Well," I said, "what happened to the two prisoners who disappeared and never were found?"

Then the warden left, slamming the door shut. There is something psychological about prison locks. The authorities want you to hear that you are locked in.

The next day, a young woman came to see me. She said she was a psychologist and wanted to discuss my "problems." I asked if she spoke Sámi. "No," she said, "but you speak Norwegian very well."

"Maybe," I said, "but I have also watched many movies, and there is always an attractive young woman sent by the authorities to get prisoners to talk. I didn't ask to see you." She started to cry and left. I felt bad, but since I had decided to play street theater, I needed to go through with it.

The following day, a Sámi doctor came. I knew him from school, and he had also been at the protests in Álttá. He said the authorities had had a hard time finding a Sámi speaker, so they decided to send him. He also told me that he knew what I was up to, and that it was a good plan. But I had to let go of the oranges; this would make things harder but also more efficient. It would make the authorities concerned. He suggested that I should tell them that I had seen someone poison the oranges. His plan was better than mine.

It didn't take long and some of my restrictions were lifted. I was allowed to go to the exercise yard. There, a man approached me. He was neither a prison officer nor a policeman, just someone with a reference from the Sámi doctor I had seen. The man offered to take me to lunch. I said that, first of all, I wouldn't eat, and, second, I was in chains. He ordered the chains to be removed and told me that we would go to a buffet lunch: I could watch other people eat and then take from the same tray. I went along with that.

For two weeks, this man and I had lunch at the same place every day, and I slowly recovered. We only ever talked about fishing and hunting and such things, until he told me one day that he had talked to the Ministry of Justice and that the officials had agreed to release me. I would remain under observation, but in no obtrusive manner. That was good news.

When I got back to the prison, my cell was already empty. Two Sámi-speaking police officers were waiting for me. One worked for the secret police. He introduced a new condition for my release: I had to tell him who the third man was on the night of the bombing. We sat down and he put a tape recorder in front of me. I commented on how lucky the Norwegian police was to have Sámi helping them. Then I told him that the third man had been Leif Halonen, a highly respected member of the Sámi Council and the Workers' Party—just about the most unlikely person to engage in such an action. The officer knew I was lying and tried to trick me: No, it couldn't have been Leif Halonen, but it might have been Veikko Holmberg, a very gentle man and dedicated activist from the Finnish side of Sápmi. I told him: "Okay, now I have lied to you, and you have lied to me. Let's stop with this nonsense, because I will never tell you who the third man was. If that means that I have to stay in prison, that's fine, because, frankly, I know there are folks out there who hate me for what I did, and it's probably safer for me in here anyway." Then I returned to my cell.

It didn't take long for the warden to appear and tell me to get out. Outside, the two police officers were waiting for me. We went by taxi to the hotel at Tromsø Airport. We were booked on a flight to Leavdnja the next day. In the morning, the officers were disappointed that I hadn't used the phone. They had told me that I could make "as many calls as I wanted." "Oh, yes, I forgot," I said. A few hours later I was home.

How did you get to Canada?
Friends got me tickets. Before the journey, I visited the *noaidi* my family had been turning to for a long time. I wanted to ask for protection. At first, he seemed very concerned. "Niillas, why do I see golden knives? What are you up to now?" When I told him about my destination—Yellowknife— he relaxed and sent me on my way: "Many will try to see you, but no one will. Just go ahead and travel!"

Where did your flight leave from?
Helsinki. I was traveling with a stolen passport. The first step was to shake off the police officers observing me.

One evening, I left the house with my car, together with my wife and sister, one of them hiding on the backseat. I knew I could lose the officers on the way to Kárášjohka, they were only driving a Ford Escort 1.6. I had a faster car. And they wouldn't recognize me driving, they would only see two people in the front seats. I drove toward Kárášjohka as fast as I could and changed into a car waiting for me along the road. My wife and my sister turned around and met the officers who followed them back to their house, assuming they had gone on a little outing.

In Kárášjohka, I dyed my hair, trying to match the photo in the passport I was using. Crossing into Finland was no problem, but at the airport in Helsinki, the immigration officer took a long look at the passport and asked, "Is this really you?"

"Of course," I smiled.

He handed me my documents and said, "Have a nice journey."

Weren't you nervous?
No, I had visited the *noaidi*. The rest of the journey went smoothly.

How were the contacts in Canada established?

Through the World Council of Indigenous Peoples. Not the organization as such, but individuals within it.

How was your arrival?
First, I had to be hidden. I was brought to Brentwood Bay on Vancouver Island. There, I stayed in a longhouse. It was a great place. There is a First Nation reserve surrounded by a colonial settlement.

One man, Phillip Paul, became my prime contact. He visited me at the longhouse regularly, trying to understand my story. I had to explain why I was white. I told him about the Álta conflict, and we talked much about spirituality. His people were just going through a phase of rediscovering their own spirituality and ceremonies.

Almost all of what I knew about Sámi spirituality I had learned during one summer, which I spent at a nursing home with my grandfather. He explained many things to me and said: "You might not understand the meaning of all of this now, but one day, when I'll be gone, you will have use for it."

Phillip Paul and I discovered that we had many things in common. We had wonderful conversations, and it became clear to him that I wasn't just some wild man in hiding. A few months later, I was adopted by the Nuxalk Nation during a ceremony in Williams Lake. After that, I stayed in Bella Coola.

When did it become known that you were in Canada?
It only took about a month. Until then, my siblings had done a good job making the authorities believe I was still in Norway. We knew our phone was tapped. But when a journalist friend, Bjarne Store-Jakobsen, wanted to visit me and make the story public, I agreed under the condition that my exact whereabouts weren't revealed. This also made it easier for my wife and our two kids to join me in Canada.

How long did you stay?
For about two years.

And this was tolerated by the Canadian authorities?
My hosts had made an agreement with them: as long as I was keeping a low profile, they wouldn't interfere. There was much

more negotiation between First Nations and Canadian authorities than between the Sámi and the Norwegian government. I wasn't used to that.

Why did you leave after two years?
My sister had gotten sick and my parents were old. It was a difficult time for the family. I felt I had to be there. Also, the charges against John Reier and me had changed. We were no longer accused of arson but of the "attempt to cause grave damage to public property." John Reier got sentenced to the prison time he had already spent in jail awaiting trial. I could expect the same, and it was unlikely that I'd have to return to prison.

When a Canadian television crew wanted to shoot a documentary about me and my family, I sought the elders' approval. We knew that this was not keeping a low profile and that it would cause the authorities to act. The elders gave me their blessing.

As soon as the film crew arrived, the police made an appearance. My hosts gathered in a circle around the house I was staying in, and, during the filming, the cops backed off. When the filming was done, I left with my friend Bjarne Store-Jakobsen, who by now was living in Canada with his partner, Esther Tailfeathers from the Kaina Nation. Their daughter, Elle-Máijá Tailfeathers, is a well-known filmmaker today. I was waiting at their mobile home to be arrested. We didn't want to cause any disturbance for the nation that had hosted me for two years. The police came in the middle of the night and, soon thereafter, we were on our way to Norway.

Why did you wait to be deported instead of just leaving the country?
Economic reasons. It was nice that the authorities paid for our trip. We had no money.

How was your return to Norway?
We survived. With the help of friends, I got work as a journalist in Sámi media.

In 1986, John Reier Martinsen was killed while driving a dogsled. He was hit by a snowmobile driven by a nineteen-year-old man from Álta. The police classified it as an accident, but there were doubts. Is this anything you can comment on?

I have thought about this a lot. At some point, I was utterly convinced that it was murder. But that's a very strong accusation to make, so I prefer not to make any claims. However, much about the case is very strange. To begin with, it seems very unlikely that someone loses control over a snowmobile, drives into a dogsled, kills the driver and six dogs, and then carries on driving. Furthermore, there are no photographs from the scene. The police said their film broke inside the camera. I worked as a photographer for a long time. Film can break inside a camera, but it's very easy to rescue it if you want to. I don't think the police was part of some conspiracy, but a cover-up is certainly a possibility.

People have to understand that the social climate around Áltá was very infected at the time. There was a lot of hatred by those who supported the dam for those who opposed it. Not only did the police use violence against protesters, but so did counterprotesters. The police usually just watched and made sure no one was taking pictures. The young man who killed John Reier might have been influenced by all that.

As a very prominent figure during the protests, what's your status in Sámi society today?
Mixed, as it has always been. There is respect, and there is rejection. I have always spoken my mind. Diplomacy is not one of my virtues. That causes strife within the Sámi community as well. But it doesn't faze me, especially now that I'm a pensioner. I can say exactly what I want. My reindeer were slaughtered a long time ago.

Metaphorically or literally?
Very literally.

Do people still call you a terrorist?
No one has called me that since Anders Behring Breivik killed seventy-seven people at a social-democratic youth camp in 2011. I assume people understand now what terrorism really is.

You mentioned the disappointment with the development of Sámi politics after the Áltá conflict. What's your impression today?
In recent years, the Norwegian state has strongly relied on the Supreme Court to keep its grip on Sápmi. The Jovsset Ánte Sara

case is one example. The state wants to remain in full control of reindeer herding. And as far as the Finnmark Act is concerned, we're still waiting for any significant impact. You can now apply for ownership of the land that you've been using traditionally for fishing, hunting, and reindeer herding. But how much good does that do if all applications are rejected? The Supreme Court has dismissed cases because the people seeking ownership of a certain area hadn't "always" lived there. By that logic, no one is ever going to qualify for anything.

In some ways, things have become more complicated because of the Finnmark Act. Before it was passed, we could go to the forest and collect firewood. Now we have to pay for it. It feels like we have given away land with the stroke of a pen, rather than ensuring that it is ours. I know of no other indigenous peoples who have done such a thing.

The Sámi Parliament has consultation rights. That is as much as it has achieved. But what are consultation rights? It means the authorities are obliged to meet with you and listen to what you have to say—before doing whatever they want to do.

There has been remarkably little militant resistance in Sámi history. Would things be different had there been more?
I'm not an advocate for militancy, even if some people see me that way. The question is not being peaceful or militant. You can be active on many levels. One that has been neglected is the spiritual level. Spiritual action is most important. People have to wake up! We need more things than language and traditional clothing to reconfirm our identity. Practicing traditional spirituality is not only about healing and medicine, it is about understanding how everything is connected, about being able to relate to nature and be its guardian.

To have a Sámi state has never been a pronounced goal among Sámi activists, but I read in an interview that you once were attracted by the idea. Can you explain?
I was naive and believed in my people. I hadn't understood how strong the impact of colonialism was. To have a Sámi state might still be a good idea, but we need to go through a process of decolonization first. One generation won't be enough. How can you

expect decolonization of a people who don't respect their own tradition?

But the tradition hasn't been lost, right?
No. This is one of the hopes I have. Also, non-Sámi begin to understand the importance of spirituality. And then there is a new generation of great Sámi artists. During the early stages of the court case against her brother, I spoke with Máren Ánne Sara. I told her that if you want to be an activist, you must not be afraid of anything. You must not care about the police or anyone else. Otherwise, you will censor yourself, you will limit your freedom, and you won't get anywhere.

Sámiland to the Sámi

Kalervo Siikala

This is an excerpt from a lecture by Kalervo Siikala on February 5, 1977, at the seventieth anniversary of the University of Helsinki student nation Pohjois-Pohjalainen Osakunta's founding. Siikala, a longtime Finnish politician, was at the time responsible for international issues at the Ministry for Education. The lecture was printed in Swedish in no. 3 (1979) of *Charta 79*. Translation by G.K.

The experience of Nordic collaboration in matters relating to the Sámi has been positive enough to now develop a comprehensive, long-term plan. Its political and legal foundation would be a pan-Nordic recognition of the Sámi as a nation and the Sámi people's constitutional protection as a minority culture in the Nordic countries. But legal protection is not enough. Economic and social rights need to be guaranteed as well. Norway, Sweden, and Finland need to give up some of their sovereignty in Fennoscandia for the benefit of a self-governed, autonomous Sámiland. This would be in line with what the United Nations expect from the countries that signed its charter, especially with respect to Article 73, which concerns the nonautonomous regions they govern over. A "sacred trust" obliges the signatory countries to ensure the welfare of the people in such regions and to develop their political institutions on the road to self-government.

Regional self-determination is nothing new in the Nordic countries. The experience of self-determination in Åland and on the Faroe Islands has been positive. The autonomy of Sámiland can be built on the same grounds.

Åland and the Faroe Islands are subjected to only one country each; Åland of Finland, and the Faroe Islands of Denmark. Sámiland would be the subjected to three countries. This will, of course, complicate things. Indeed, it is the main reason why Sámi self-determination has so far seemed impossible. Yet the development of the pan-Nordic institutions, the Nordic Council and the Nordic Council of Ministers, has made an agreement on Sámiland between the concerned countries possible. Such an agreement could provide the same protection and support of Sámiland that federal governments provide for the indigenous peoples of the Arctic in Canada and the Soviet Union. In my view, it would be beneficial if Iceland and Denmark were part of such an arrangement. Denmark has once governed parts of the Sámi territory and could, together with Iceland, occupy the role of a neutral mediator should conflicts between Norway, Sweden, and Finland arise concerning the development of Sámiland.

As far as the borders of Sámiland are concerned, the governments of Finland and Sweden have already defined particular Sámi areas, even if the criteria used were different. This has not yet happened in Norway, but as it is the country where the majority of the Sámi population lives, demographic statistics can be used as guidelines. In many of the municipalities of northern Norway, the Sámi constitute a majority.

Sámiland can never be monolingual and home to only one nation, but I don't think that this would be desirable either. An important aspect of life in Fennoscandia has always been a certain cosmopolitan freedom with open borders, and this must remain. The rights of the non-Sámi population can be secured by legislation similar to that protecting the rights of the Swedish-speaking population in Finland. The rights of non-Sámi who are engaged in Sámi industries—reindeer herding, small-scale agriculture, fishing, and so on—are directly linked to the interests of the Sámi vis-à-vis external interests represented by state authorities, corporations, and tourism.

In education and culture, it is relatively easy to achieve autonomy based on the Sámi's growing national identity and the advancement of a related Sámi-conscious class among the population. Economic and environmental questions must also be part of Sámi autonomy, however. Fennoscandia is under serious pressure from our industrial-commercial system. The exploitation of oil and natural gas along the coast of the Arctic Ocean, announced by the prime ministers of Norway, Sweden, and Finland, will multiply this pressure over the coming decades. Both the social structures of Sámiland and its fragile, vulnerable nature might not survive this pressure. The half-colonialism that has been exercised in Fennoscandia for decades has reached its utter limit.

Who in the Nordic countries can have an interest in the destruction of Europe's last wilderness area? Who can be willing to sacrifice the preconditions for the indigenous people, the Sámi, to survive to the altar of economic growth and entertainment? What kind of conscience allows us to preach freedom and equality when we ignore the slow agony of an entire people at our doorstep, the far north of Europe?

Top: "Let the river live!" Protest camp at Nullpunktet during the Áltá crisis, 1981 (Hans Ove Tverrfjell/Alta Museum). Bottom: activists chaining themselves together during the protests against the Áltá-Guovdageaidnu River dam, 1979 (Arne Eriksen/Alta Museum).

Top: protest camp outside the Parliament of Norway during the Álta crisis.
Bottom: "We want to protect our land: Sámiland." Protest in Oslo during the
Álta crisis. Synnøve Persen inside the *lávvu* (both Niillas Somby).

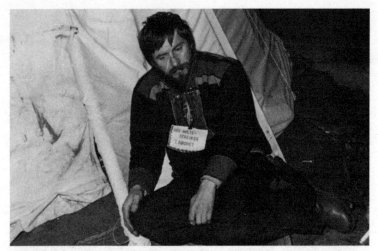

Top: Niillas Somby during the 1979 hunger strike. The sign says: "I am on hunger strike, day seven." (Courtesy of Niillas Somby.) Bottom: the Sámi women who occupied the Norwegian prime minister's office in 1981 (D.M. Sørensen/Ája, Jåhkåmåhke).

Left: activist removed by police at Nullpunkten during the Áltá protests, 1981 (Hans Ove Tjerfell/Alta Museum). Bottom: in January 1981, the passenger ship *Janina* arrived in Áltá, equipped to house six hundred Norwegian police officers (Frode Pedersen/Alta Museum).

Left: Niillas Somby barbecuing salmon in Canada (Anja Karin Somby). Bottom: Niillas Somby (far right) with his daughters Risten and Anja Karin, his former wife Dagny Elisabet, Nuxalx Chief Lawrence Pootlas, and Amalie Pootlas in Bella Coola, 1983 (Keith Pootlas).

Left: Áltá-Guovdageaidnu River dam, 2003 (Bair175/ Wikimedia Commons). Bottom: "Somby Bridge," 2012 (Carl-Magnus Helgegren/ Wikimedia Commons).

Ann-Kristin Håkansson

Source: ITU

Ann-Kristin Håkansson (born 1950) has been a Sámi delegate in various international organizations, including the World Council for Indigenous Peoples and the Indigenous ICT Task Force. She has worked in both United Nations and European Union projects on indigenous peoples. Ann-Kristin is a board member of the Stockholm-based indigenous peoples solidarity group Fjärde Världen (Fourth World). We spoke in Stockholm during the summer of 2019.

In 1975, the World Council of Indigenous Peoples (WCIP) was founded at a conference in Port Alberni on Vancouver Island, British Columbia. A Sámi delegation was present. Who appointed the delegates?
The Sámi Council. It was also the Sámi Council who took on the responsibility to organize the second WCIP conference in Giron in 1977. It was an inspiring event.

Who funded the conference?
The governments of Norway, Sweden, and Finland all contributed. The Canadian government contributed as well. The initiator of the WCIP had been the National Indian Brotherhood, a forerunner to the present-day Assembly of First Nations.

In 1979, the WCIP was granted the status of nongovernmental organization by the United Nations Economic and Social Council. Did this have a big impact on its activities?
No, none at all. It just meant that we had access to UN resources.

After that, there were a couple more conferences, one in Canberra in 1981, and one in Romsa in 1990. A few years later, the WCIP dissolved. What happened?
It's an old story: as soon as funding is coming in, things get complicated. Money disappeared, there was corruption . . . It was an unpleasant situation for everyone.

Why has there never been a successor organization?
There were attempts, but nothing ever materialized. It's a very unfortunate story. Most of us who experienced that time feel that we missed a unique opportunity. There was never a better time to unite the global indigenous movement.

Why?
The 1970s were a decade of optimism, indigenous people were active across the globe, and everyone was keen on establishing international contacts.

Do you still keep in touch with other WCIP delegates?

Yes, loosely. I still feel there needs to be an evaluation of what happened, not least to understand the situation we find ourselves in now.

In the early 2000s, you got involved in the Indigenous ICT Task Force within the International Telecommunications Union (ITU), a UN agency. Can you tell us about that?
The task force came out of the World Summits on the Information Society in Geneva, 2003, and Tunis, 2005. Kenneth Deer from the Mohawk Nation was supposed to attend but couldn't. He asked me to go instead and lobby for the needs of indigenous peoples.

It was interesting because these conferences weren't about indigenous issues at all. We had to bring questions to the table that were of relevance to us, everything from indigenous languages to internet access in remote areas. We were able to raise awareness about indigenous issues in an arena where there had been none. I considered this a big success.

Unfortunately, there are always nonindigenous persons in such organizations who feel the need to lead, even if they know nothing about indigenous peoples and their needs.

Based on your experiences with the UN and its agencies: how much can they help indigenous peoples in asserting their rights?
Not much. First of all, everything takes forever. Before the UN Resolution on the Rights of Indigenous Peoples was passed in 2007, a working group was preparing it for twenty-five years. And UN resolutions aren't even binding. They might put some pressure on nation-state governments, but their actual influence is weak.

You have also worked with the European Union.
My overall impressions there were better. There was genuine interest for indigenous questions, both by the European Commission and the EU Parliament. Some of it might be due to the fact that few European countries have to deal with resistance by indigenous peoples, but still . . . EU representatives were open to talk and followed our demand that projects concerning indigenous people were to be led by indigenous people only. However, in terms of forcing state governments to change their policies, the powers of the EU are limited as well.

When we speak of indigenous peoples' rights, what are issues that seem particularly pressing today?
Intellectual property rights is a burning question.

Can you explain?
Traditional knowledge, cultural expression, and genetic resources are the final things that the colonizers are taking away from indigenous people. The colonizers want everything. Massive education programs are required to protect indigenous people from this exploitation. Most of them know nothing about copyright or public domain. Many are just glad if someone, finally, wants to listen to them; they share their knowledge about everything from herbs and natural medicines to unique forms of art and handicraft.

It's not that indigenous people shouldn't share what they know with others, but sharing isn't a one-way street. The benefits need to be shared as well. Indigenous people have long lived in poverty, generation after generation. This needs to change.

There has been some progress. People have been taken to court for exploiting indigenous art, and earlier this year Nike was forced to drop a sneaker that was using indigenous designs. On the other hand, you have outsiders who register a patent for certain indigenous designs. There is a case in Sápmi right now where the German husband of a Sámi woman has registered a patent on an ancient solar symbol. He is now suing Sámi artists using it in their work. It's absurd.

Everyone is still talking about human rights, but discussions about human rights can become very abstract. Discussions about intellectual property rights, on the other hand, are very concrete.

If you look back at all of the international projects and organizations you've been involved with: how much has been achieved?
Too little.

Why?
It's easy to create a bubble. People travel from conference to conference, but they are only meeting among themselves. There is too much mingling and too little outreach. There is also a lack of strategy. Look at what other organizations can do. Share experiences!

We also need to get away from the shopping lists of causes we claim to support, promising improvements for all sorts of underprivileged communities. But the problems of indigenous peoples aren't necessarily the same as those of LGBT persons or people with special needs. We need specific agendas for specific causes.

I also see troubling developments within indigenous movements. A couple of years ago, a longtime fellow activist from Gárasavvon and I traveled to the annual session of the United Nations Permanent Forum on Indigenous Issues in New York. There was a youth caucus, and we wanted to listen to what the young activists' concerns were. It was made very clear to us that we weren't welcome. It was the first time I witnessed elders being excluded from an indigenous setting.

How much is the struggle of the Sámi affected by four different nation-states occupying their territories?
Of course it affects us. We fight together and by ourselves at the same time.

You've worked for the Sámi Council, which includes Sámi from all sides of Sápmi. How do you see the relationship between the council and the Sámi parliaments?
I feel there is too much overlap. We have people who are members of both the Sámi Council and a Sámi parliament. But these institutions should be kept apart. The Sámi parliaments are integrated into the national political structure. The Sámi Council is a transnational body to strengthen the rights of the Sámi people. You can easily have conflicts of interest.

The Sámi parliaments don't have much political power. Should Sámi politicians be more involved in the political institutions of the nation-state they live in?
I have always demanded Sámi seats in the Swedish Parliament. This is the only way we will ever get influence on national politics. To climb through the ranks of the political parties is a dead end. Not a single Sámi has succeeded, even within the parties that present themselves as Sámi-friendly, like the Greens.

I asked Niillas Somby about an independent Sámi state as a solution, being aware that this has never been a demand by any Sámi organization or movement. What are your thoughts?

People can have all sorts of dreams, but such a demand would mean political suicide. There is no chance of getting there. We need to focus on strong autonomy rights.

How can they be implemented?

The structures are in place. If the Sámi parliaments get actual political power and control over Sápmi's natural resources, we will have come a long way.

Declaration of Principles

World Council of Indigenous Peoples

This document was adopted by the General Assembly of the World Council of Indigenous Peoples at a gathering in Panama City, Panama, 1984.

1. All human rights of indigenous people must be respected. No form of discrimination against indigenous people shall be allowed.

2. All indigenous peoples have the right to self-determination. By virtue of this right they can freely determine their political, economic, social, religious and cultural development, in agreement with the principles stated in this declaration.

3. Every nation-state within which indigenous peoples live shall recognize the population, territory and institutions belonging to said peoples.

4. The culture of indigenous peoples is part of mankind's cultural patrimony.

5. The customs and usages of the indigenous peoples must be respected by the nation-states and recognized as a legitimate source of rights.

6. Indigenous peoples have the right to determine which person(s) or group(s) is (are) included in its population.

7. All indigenous peoples have the right to determine the form, structure and jurisdiction of their own institutions.

8. The institutions of indigenous peoples, like those of a nation-state, must conform to internationally recognized human rights, both individual and collective.

9. Indigenous peoples, and their individual members, have the right to participate in the political life of the nation-state in which they are located.

10. Indigenous peoples have inalienable rights over their traditional lands and resources. All lands and resources which have been usurped, or taken away without the free and knowledgeable consent of indigenous peoples, shall be restored to them.

11. The rights of the indigenous peoples to their lands include the soil, the subsoil, coastal economic zones all within the limits specified by international legislation.

12. All indigenous peoples have the right to freely use their natural wealth and resources in order to satisfy their needs, and in agreement with principles 10 and 11 above.

13. No action or process shall be implemented which directly and/or indirectly would result in the destruction of land, air, water, glaciers, animal life, environment or natural resources, without the free and well informed consent of the affected indigenous peoples.

14. Indigenous peoples will re-assume original rights over their material culture, including archeological zones, artifacts, designs and other artistic expressions.

15. All indigenous peoples have the right to be educated in their own language and to establish their own education institutions. Indigenous peoples' languages shall be respected by nation-states in all dealings between them on the basis of equality and nondiscrimination.

16. All treaties reached through agreement between indigenous peoples and representatives of the nation-states will have total validity before national and international law.

17. Indigenous peoples have the right, by virtue of their traditions, to freely travel across international boundaries, to conduct traditional activities and maintain family links.

18. Indigenous peoples and their designated authorities have the right to be consulted and to authorize the implementation of technological and scientific research conducted within their territories and the right to be informed about the results of such activities.

19. The aforementioned principles constitute the minimal rights to which indigenous peoples are entitled and must be complemented by all nation-states.

Øyvind Ravna

Photo courtesy of Øyvind Ravna

Øyvind Ravna (born 1961) is a law professor at the University of Tromsø—Arctic University of Norway. From 1988 to 2004, he worked as a land consolidation judge in Finnmark County. Apart from numerous publications on law and Sámi rights in Norway, Øyvind has written on the Lakota and on Arctic life in Russia. He is a passionate photographer, and many of his publications are lavishly illustrated. For more information, see www.ravna.no. We talked via video stream in August 2019.

Out of the nation-states governing different parts of Sápmi, only Norway has ratified the ILO Convention 169. How much of a difference does that make? Or does it mainly look good on paper?
It probably looks better on paper than it does in practice. But of course it makes a difference. ILO 169 demands to recognize indigenous peoples' rights to ownership of the land they have been traditionally using. That changes the legal framework. However, it doesn't answer the question of implementation. It is important to differentiate between two things: *ratifying* an international convention means that a government commits itself to honoring its contents; *incorporating* an international convention means to actually make it part of national law. In Norway, there has been what's called "sectorial incorporation" of ILO 169 through the 2005 Finnmark Act. The act has been adopted to meet the requirements under ILO 169, but there's an issue here: the only demand by the Supreme Court of Norway is that the wording of the Finnmark Act does not contradict ILO 169. Consequently, ILO 169 does not determine the legal investigations foreseen by the act.

What are the act's most important points?
The Finnmark Act has transferred all of the land in Finnmark County formerly owned by the state—about 95 percent of the entire land area—to the people of Finnmark.

How does this play out in practice?
The administration of the land is now in the hands of a body called the "Finnmark Estate," Finnmarkseiendommen in Norwegian, or Finnmárkkuopmodat in North Sámi. It is often abbreviated as FeFo. FeFo's board consists of three members appointed by the Sámi Parliament and three appointed by the Finnmark County Council. Of particular importance, however, is the "Finnmark Commission," Finnmarkskommisjonen in Norwegian, or Finnmárkokomišuvdna in North Sámi. This is the body that investigates the rights of use and ownership of the land, for example when Sámi claim rights based on the traditional use of certain areas for reindeer herding, hunting, or fishing. So far, however, not a single square meter has been identified as Sámi collective property.

How is that possible?

The commission is meant to base its decisions on three criteria: the *use* of the land, the *duration* of its use, and whether it was used in "*good faith*," meaning that the people who used it were unaware of violating someone else's property rights. But the "good faith," in particular, is very hard to prove. All of the land was formally owned by the state up to 2005, and pretty much everyone knew this. So how do you prove that you were using it in "good faith"? Emphasizing heavily the previous state ownership, the courts have set legal standards that are hard to turn around.

It sounds as if, on the ground, nothing has changed at all since the Finnmark Act has come into effect.
That's more or less true. However, the areas around Guovdageaidnu and Kárášjohka, the heartland of the Sámi people, have not been surveyed yet, so we don't know what's going to be the result there. But it's not like the Sámi along the coast didn't have good reasons to claim traditional ownership of their territories. It's not been a very encouraging start for them.

Are court cases part of everyday life for the Sámi community?
There are many legal procedures, yes.

What are the most common issues ending up in court?
Most cases are about the land and concern reindeer herding. Last year, there was a well-publicized case in Norway regarding wind power on reindeer pastures, as the government plans to build Europe's biggest land-based wind farm in the district of Fosen, near Tråante. We can expect more such cases in the future. Everything that concerns land is contentious. Language rights, and cultural rights in general, are easier to be granted. They appear less dangerous.

As I understand, the cases don't very often go the Sámi's way.
That is true. And the situation has worsened in recent years, at least in Norway.

Why?
Difficult to say. The political climate is not supportive of the Sámi just now. The judicial system ought to be independent as the third

state power, but it seems to be colored by the political streams in the country.

One recent case has received particular attention in Norway: reindeer herder Jovsset Ánte Sara's refusal to cull the majority of his reindeer, as demanded by the Norwegian Ministry of Agriculture and Food. Why has it been covered widely? I assume the solidarity campaign driven by Jovsset Ánte's sister, the well-known artist Marét Anné Sara, is one reason. What are others?

Jovsset Ánte Sara's case is quite extreme. He is a young reindeer herder who doesn't have a huge herd yet. If he culls all the reindeer requested by the authorities, he'd be down to seventy-five animals. But you can't make a living off seventy-five reindeer. Furthermore, both the district court and the court of appeal, the first two instances of Norway's judiciary, ruled in Jovsset Ánte Sara's favor. In other words, the decision by the Ministry of Agriculture and Food was considered unlawful, also with regard to standards set by the United Nations Human Rights Committee. The Supreme Court overturned the decision. Finally, there is a cruel irony involved here: only a few years ago, Jovsset Ánte Sara received state subsidies for building a herd and establishing himself as a reindeer herder—and now he's supposed to slaughter most of them.

Jovsset Ánte Sara has now taken the case to the UN Human Rights Committee.

He argues that his rights as a member of a minority culture are violated, as the forced cull would mean he'd be unable to work as a reindeer herder and maintain a key element of Sámi culture. It will be very interesting to see the what the committee has to say and what the consequences for reindeer herding will be.

Is it common that reindeer herders take the government to court in a case of forced culling?

No.

Why not?

You pay a high price. Jovsset Ánte Sara will probably be in debt for the rest of his life, as he's slapped with a fine for every day he delays the cull.

In Norway and Sweden, Sámi own the exclusive right to reindeer herding, but not in Finland. Does that make a big difference in terms of government control?

Finnish legislation might be more flexible in terms of ownership, but reindeer herding must still be a livelihood and all government regulations apply. It's not like anyone can come and start herding reindeer as they wish.

You have also done work on the Russian side of Sápmi. Is the situation there in any way comparable to that of the Nordic countries?

Not really—at least not when focusing on law. There's been a different history and the current political situation is different, too. It's difficult to have a discussion specifically about Sámi rights when the civil rights of the entire population are under threat. Russia is not a democratic country, and protest is brutally suppressed. This, of course, has a very negative impact on the situation of the Sámi there, too.

Speaking of comparing situations: you wrote a book about the Lakota in Norwegian. The title translates as "From Little Bighorn to Standing Rock." Why this topic?

I have always been interested in the subject. When a sabbatical made it possible for me to do research in the US, I decided to do a book. The history is very interesting from a Sámi perspective, not least concerning the legal implications. In North America, there is a lot of talk about broken treaties. In Sápmi, we never had any treaties. The nation-state governments just expanded into the Sámi areas, step by step. At the same time, the oppression of indigenous people never reached the level it did in North America, where, under today's international conventions, one might speak of a genocide.

How important is comparative research for indigenous scholars?

Very. If I didn't think so, I wouldn't have spent so much time doing it. It deepens your knowledge, you learn to understand the problems of other indigenous peoples better, and, perhaps most importantly, you learn about the ways they have been trying to solve them.

You were at the protests against the Dakota Access Pipeline at Standing Rock. What were your impressions?

I was there more as an observer than an active participant, but I was very impressed by the number of people who gathered, many of whom had traveled long distances. The sense of community was overwhelming. But I was also shocked by the police violence I witnessed toward the end of 2016. When Trump got elected, there was a whole new momentum.

I talked to Ann-Kristin Håkansson about how there hasn't been a successor organization to the World Council of Indigenous Peoples. What are your thoughts on the future of organizing the international indigenous movement?

I think that the United Nations Permanent Forum on Indigenous Issues and other international bodies, such as the Arctic Council, provide a useful infrastructure. The problem is that, today, the influence of these institutions is decreasing rather than increasing. The situation is similar with regard to human rights: they do not have sufficient influence on lawmaking these days. We see this not just with regard to indigenous peoples but in many areas: migration, war, deforestation in the Amazon. I'm not sure what the solution is. We live in difficult times politically, and that also affects indigenous organizing.

The Norwegian Hunger Games

This is an accompanying text to Máret Ánne Sara's painting "The Norwegian Hunger Games" (see full-color insert), taken from the website www.maretannesara.com.

The Norwegian Hunger Games, 2016: A part of Sara's work related to Pile o'Sápmi and the "Oaivemozit/Madness/Galskap" series from 2013. A visual portrait of how the Norwegian government's model of the forced reindeer cullings are affecting the Sámi society internally.

The Norwegian authorities have set a maximum number of reindeer in northern Norway, based on calculations of optimal meat production. This means that a certain percentage of the total reindeer population is to be slaughtered in the largest Sámi reindeer herding area. Officially, the Norwegian government claims that the Sámi reindeer herders had—and exercised—self-determination in the reduction process. This so-called "inner self-determination" came into effect only after the government had set the total number of animals to be slaughtered, leaving the reindeer herders only to decide who amongst the reindeer herders was going to slaughter and how much. Any internal reduction model by the reindeer herders was only accepted if it was a unanimous agreement, signed by all reindeer herders representing a *siida*-share. A *siida*-share includes many reindeer herders or reindeer owners within a family, meaning that any *siida*-share had to agree internally on a reduction-split before negotiating with the other *siida*-share representatives in the district. This so called "inner self-determination" has left people quarreling over private properties of each other, and ultimately also over fundamental cultural rights of individuals. Not surprisingly, this effort achieved little results but caused high level of stress and internal conflicts—and lawsuits within the reindeer herding society and families.

Once herders failed to meet the impossible requirements of unanimously signed agreements, it was officially stated that the reindeer herders are "incapable" of self-determination and the government formally legitimized an overtaking of the process of setting a forced reduction model. The forced reduction model implemented by the government required all *siida*-shares within a district to slaughter the same percentage of their herd, regardless of how many reindeer each individual *siida*-share had initially. The process was effectively a form of collective punishment—disproportionately affecting the smallest herds, such as those of young herders establishing themselves, and thus also recruitment into the traditional livelihood.

Before implementing the forced reduction process, the Norwegian Parliament unilaterally modified the national Reindeer Herding Act, adding a whole chapter about legal punishments and forced measures against herders who do not voluntarily slaughter their herds down to the level the government has determined as "sustainable." These constitutional changes were made despite strong objections from the Sámi Parliament and the Norwegian Sámi Reindeer Herding Association.

Mari Boine

Photo: Göran Fors/www.goranfors.com

Mari Boine (born 1956) is an internationally renowned recording artist, blending the musical heritage of Sápmi with elements from various other musical traditions. A tireless advocate for Sámi rights, Mari is often described as an ambassador for her people. She has cowritten the score for the Nils Gaup movie *The Kautokeino Rebellion* (2008) and received numerous Sámi and Norwegian awards for her musical oeuvre. For detailed information, see www.mariboine.no. I visited Mari at her home in Porsáŋgu in June 2019.

In *Den stille kampen* (The Silent Struggle), a Norwegian TV series about Sámi history, you talked about how shy and withdrawn you were when you were younger. Today, you are Sápmi's most renowned recording artist and often referred to as an unofficial "Sámi ambassador." That sounds like quite a journey.

Yes, it's been quite a journey. Sometimes, when I look back, I wonder where I got the courage from. I was *very* shy as a child and a young woman. When I studied at the teacher's training college, I was still afraid that the professor would ask my opinion. I felt I had no opinion.

A current neighbor of mine, who I went to school with when we were sixteen, was among the students who were always on stage. Something I would have never dared to do. When I finally did appear on stage, at the age of twenty-four, she was studying in Bergen, in the south of Norway. She came to three or four of my concerts before she realized who I was. She couldn't imagine this woman on stage being me. It illustrates how much I changed, but it also proves how much there can be hidden inside shy people.

Today, you feel comfortable with your role?

I have always felt safe on stage. I could feel unsafe in everyday life, socializing was difficult for me. But the stage was my home from the very beginning. I felt nobody could touch me there.

But you also have to deal with the media and appear at public events. Isn't that difficult?

Not so much. I have learned to play that role. In our culture, we believe in helpers. When I look back, I can see that I've always had helpers. I like to think that there was a wise old woman who started to whisper songs in my ear when I was young. And then she told me, "You have to go on stage, girl!" I said, "No, no, find someone else!" But in our culture some children are chosen, so I guess I had no choice.

Elders are very important in all indigenous cultures. Traditionally, when they saw something special in a child, they were preparing them for a special path. My personal journey has also been a spiritual journey. Unfortunately, this tradition has been broken in our culture. In the last decades, there has been a lot of searching in the dark.

I will be sixty-three this year. Now I am one of the elders. I like where I'm at in life. It makes many things easier. I no longer have the fears that I had when I was younger.

Do you feel responsibility as an elder?
Yes. The last time I traveled on the plane from Leavdnja to Romsa, I met another elder, a reindeer herder and a journalist. He told me that he was ready to stop writing, he felt that his voice was no longer important. I said, "No, you're wrong, you need to write a book! The young people need us." He was part of a group founding a Sámi association in Bergen in the 1960s, and so on. He would have plenty of stories to tell. Our young people need guides. I would have needed one. In the strict Læstadian community I grew up in our old ways were rejected.

Let me ask you about Læstadianism, because it seems there are two diverging interpretations: on the one hand, it is portrayed as a Pietist sect that destroyed Sámi culture and, on the other, as a Sámi adaptation of Christianity that gave Sámi pride and strengthened their identity. How do the two go together?
It is true that both sides exist. I only experienced the Pietist one, but later I met people from Læstadian communities who felt that their faith had given them the strength to rebel against authorities.

I think the Guovdageaidnu Rebellion had a strong impact on Læstadian history. Many Sámi were shocked by the violence and felt ashamed. They never wanted their children to be part of anything similar, to stand up against the church and the government. For my father, it was very important that we were good Christians and that we had left the old ways behind. I only learned about the real history of the Guovdageaidnu Rebellion when I made the music for Nils Gaup's film. Before that, I had never heard a story other than the rebels having been crazy.

I mentioned your ambassador role. How important have the many international connections been that you have made, both for you personally and for Sámi society?
Once I realized that I had this wonderful gift, my voice, I knew I had to travel abroad and be successful. I knew how strong the psychological effect would be on my people. Sámi society was

full of self-hatred caused by colonization when I began singing. People told me to sing in Norwegian, because they felt that the Sámi language had no value. For the Sámi in Norway, Oslo and the Norwegian government were the center of the world. I remember when I played at the Roskilde Festival in Denmark in the 1980s, during one of my first tours. I was looking for Norwegian newspapers, because I wanted to see whether they had written something about my concert. When I went to a shop and asked for one, the newsagent almost seemed offended: "We don't carry Norwegian papers!" she told me. What a moment of freedom! "Finally, Norway doesn't exist," I thought.

Speaking about concerts abroad: in 2005, you performed at the opening of Kola Sámi Radio in Lujávri, Russia. Can you tell us about that experience? The Sámi community in Russia was very isolated during the twentieth century.
It was an emotional concert for both me and my Sámi brothers and sisters there. I felt a lot of love, warmth, and appreciation from the people. The isolation has been hard for them. Every time I have played in Murmánska, I also got this feeling of unity and appreciation.

On your latest album, *See the Woman*, almost all the lyrics are in English. Some were written by John Trudell and Joy Harjo. How important has the influence of Native American artists been on your work?
I first discovered Buffy Sainte-Marie, who was a huge inspiration. Then I read about the American Indian Movement, which made a big impact as well—not only on me, but on many Sámi activists.

The first time I got in contact with Native Americans was in 1988, when I attended a conference called "Off the High Horse" in Bavaria. The organizers had invited indigenous artists and activists as well as Europeans. I felt the Native Americans were rather cold toward me, and I didn't understand why—until I realized that they didn't see me as an indigenous person, they saw me as a white European. But when I got to sing, things turned around completely. They all came to me. My musical heritage had made a connection.

Since 1991, the Riddu Riđđu Festival for indigenous music and culture has been held near Romsa. Buffy Sainte-Marie is headlining

this year, and you've performed several times. How important is the festival?

Very important, as it strengthens our connections. The Sámi have more in common with other indigenous peoples than with Norwegians or other Europeans. It's also important to show the variety of indigenous culture. I have heard many times that I wasn't "Sámi enough," because there are influences from other cultures in my music. But it's all tied together.

You had to deal with criticism like that?

Oh, I had to deal with a lot. I mentioned self-hatred before. If you come from an oppressed community and claim your space, there are always people who want to hold you back. After a show in 1993, a Danish anthropologist who had been working among the Inuit in Greenland approached me and said, "I wish to God that you'll have the strength to continue on this path!" I didn't really understand what he meant. I felt I was just a singer.

Now, twenty-five years later, I do understand. I had to deal with envy, ridicule, disregard, insults, even forms of aggressive behavior. It wasn't always easy, but over time it got better. If you stick to your path, people will give in at some point and even support you. However, I still wish there had been someone to prepare me for it.

Let me return to that conference in Bavaria one more time. There I learned that spirituality isn't the same as Christianity. I'm a very spiritual person, but I don't see myself as a Christian. It was at that conference that I, for the very first time, met people who said, "I will pray for you," but who were no Christians. I was very naive and this was a new experience for me—one I am still very grateful for!

There is one woman I remember particularly well. She was over eighty years old, and her first name was Alice. I don't remember the rest of her name, but I still carry a photo of her. She gave a talk about spirituality and about how important the Creator was to her. She also told us that she had never traveled anywhere with a US passport, only with a passport issued by her own nation, no matter how much confusion that caused among immigration officers. I was very impressed. I only met this woman for a couple of days, but she became a spiritual guide to me.

On your very first album, there's a Sámi version of John Lennon's "Working Class Hero." Why did you translate those lyrics?
It's not an actual translation. I used the first poem I ever wrote and put it to John Lennon's music, because I felt that the poem fit the song's message. I wrote about a Sámi child in a Norwegian school, and about the brainwashing and the contempt for Sámi culture that they experienced. At that time, I was working as a teacher in Porsáŋgu and was in a band with some colleagues and friends. We played in local venues, and there was a man I knew to be among those who drank a lot and whom others looked down upon. One time, after we had played the song, he approached me with tears in his eyes and said, "You are singing about me." That night, I understood that the songs I wrote weren't just about me. It was an important moment for my songwriting.

In 1994, you were invited to take part in the opening ceremony of the Winter Olympics in Lillehammer. You declined. Why?
While touring in Canada earlier, I had read about the 1988 Winter Olympics and how indigenous people didn't want to serve as a decoration for the event. So when the Winter Olympics came to Norway, I thought, "Okay, now they'll want us as a decoration!"
It was a very difficult time for me personally. My parents had died, and I was going through a divorce. I wasn't feeling very strong. But I knew that if I said yes to the invitation, I had to be strong, because it is always a struggle to get these things right, to make people understand that it needs to be done in a respectful way. I felt I didn't have the energy, and so I said no.
I guess I also wanted to send a message to the Norwegian government, making it clear that they didn't respect Sámi rights enough. The government was shocked. A minister publicly declared that I was "arrogant." My response was clear: "If I was a Norwegian minister, I would never dare to use the word 'arrogant' when talking about a Sámi."

Instead of you, Nils-Aslak Valkeapää took part in the ceremony.
Yes, I thought that was kind of strange. But he felt strong enough to be there.

Was it done in a respectful way?

Well, it was exotifying. Nils-Aslak was there with a reindeer and in traditional Sámi dress. But it was good that there was a yoik. Nils-Aslak was a real yoiker, which I wasn't at the time. And the yoik he performed was strong. I think that it was good that he was there.

Cultural integration often comes more easily than the improvement of rights and living conditions. There is often a gap. How have you dealt with this throughout your career?
It's always complicated. How much of our beautiful culture do we allow them to use for their own interests? We have plenty of things they can use as decoration. Is that better than not to be seen at all? The gap always exists: they take the beauty of the culture, but they don't want to deal with us as people. As an indigenous artist, you always have to be aware and awake, which can be exhausting. And there are also those who think, "Let's not be too political; let's just be happy that our art is getting out there." There is no easy solution. But I should also add that, with regard to living conditions, the Sámi in Norway are much better off than most indigenous people in the world.

How much has the need to be aware and awake affected your artistic creation?
I always did what I wanted to do but was routinely placed in the "Sámi artist" category. That was one of the reasons why I wanted to do See the Woman, a pop album in English. I wanted to challenge the category that people placed me in and see what would happen. It was a bit like research. And people were indeed very confused. In Berlin, a journalist told me, "When I first got the CD, I thought they had given me the wrong one."

I got an honorary award at Spellemannprisen, the Norwegian Grammys, which I really appreciate, but my album wasn't nominated. I guess they didn't know what to do with it.

There are many prominent women artists in Sápmi. Do you have an explanation?
Not really, but I'd like to think that it relates to a culture in which goddesses play an important role. And if you look at Tacitus's description of the Sámi, he writes about strange people where "even the women go hunting." That always made me proud, feeling

like I was coming from a culture with strong women. But I think that colonization and Christianity ruined much of this. My mother was very strong, but she had to appear weak. In European culture, the man has to take the lead. Læstadius allowed his own daughter to preach—it's just that we were never told.

Let me return to your interview in *Den stille kampen*. At the very end, you tell an anecdote about visiting a Sámi school in Leavdnja. The students had read and discussed your lyrics and said they understood that you had felt ashamed as a Sámi growing up, but that they couldn't relate because they weren't feeling any shame. This, you concluded, showed that some progress had been made.

I think I tried to do two things during my career: strengthen my own people and educate Norwegians. I'm not sure I was very successful with respect to the latter, but I do see that my own people have become stronger, especially the youth. They wear Sámi clothes, they sing in Sámi, they yoik; they don't feel any shame, and they don't allow anyone to put them down. Look at young artists like Ella Marie Hætta Isaksen, the "new Mari Boine," as some like to call her. Ella Marie is wonderful, and she is fearless. If they want to open a new mine she'll be there in chains, she says. Yes, there has been progress.

On Mari Boine's rendition of "This Is My Heart"

Joy Harjo

Posted on Joy Harjo's Facebook page on September 2, 2016.

Listening to the raw, unmixed version of my song "This is My Heart" sung by Mari Boine, the Saami singer whom I met years ago in Saami country. Her recording of "This is My Heart" is beautiful. I've always admired her voice, her music. It's an honor for her to take my song into her breath and infuse it with yoik. Mari's voice is the open heart as it walks to the edge of possibility in song, though it has been abandoned and found love over and over again.

So much emerges as I listen. My song has found its way to Saamiland, which is now in what's known as Norway, and other Scandinavian countries. It's a way to give back to what that country and those people have given to me. I want to especially thank the Saami scholar and visionary Harald Gaski who opened the path. Mvto.

I hear my mother's songwriting. I hear her grandmother on the trail of tears. I hear my father and understand how he got caught up in bars, in the drinking culture. I was attracted to it when I was young. Each song on the jukebox or by the band was like a stepping stone for my heart to cross a river of pain. I found another way with creating art, writing poetry, and when I was forty by writing songs. My voice found its way to singing so much later, with the help of my saxophone.

For years I have struggled with music, the making of music and then finding a place for it. I have moved forward without backing from the industry, without professional assistance to promote my music. I have learned to hire the best when I take my songs to a studio and get chances to perform live. And I go out in the world in my own way, plain in jeans and shirt, to present my poetry and music. I often feel like I don't fit or belong anywhere, not even in my own family, not native music, not in any recognizable stream of American music or poetry, but I keep walking—I continue to attempt to take care of what I have been given and I admit, sometimes I give up. The river sometimes floods the banks.

Listening to Mari sing reminds me that sometimes you can't really hear what you are doing in a poem or a song until someone else gives it back to you. Songs and poems are innately restless. They like to keep moving. Mvto/thank you Mari, and to those who continue to sing, make music, and write poetry to carry us past the whirlpools of human suffering toward understanding.

Harald Gaski

Photo: Bjørn Hatteng, UiT

Harald Gaski (born 1955) is a professor of Sámi literature at Sámi allasku-vla, the Sámi University of Applied Sciences in Guovdageaidnu, and at the University of Tromsø—Arctic University of Norway. He has authored numerous books and articles on Sámi literature, culture, and politics and has translated the works from renowned Sámi poets such as Nils-Aslak Valkeapää. Harald has been a central figure in bringing together indig-enous peoples from around the world since the 1970s. We sat down for a talk in Deanušaldi in June 2019.

I'd like to begin with a question about language: are there different Sámi languages, or is there one Sámi language with different dialects?

I belong to the group who speaks of one language and different dialects. I do this for political reasons. It is obvious that we share the same culture across Sápmi, the yoik, many stories and myths, and so forth. We also find the same words all across Sápmi, even if the language has developed differently, or kept different characteristics, in certain areas due to the vast distances. I understand that calling a Sámi dialect a language in its own right can bring it more attention. North Sámi, the language spoken by the majority of Sámi, has been rather dominant and other dialects have been neglected. But still, the question is whether we want to stress the unity or the diversity of Sámi culture. I think that unity is very important. We don't need to focus on divisions.

Practically all Sámi speakers are also fully proficient in either Norwegian, Swedish, Finnish, or Russian, and English is also increasingly used, not only for international communication but between Sámi communities as well. The Sámi live in highly multilingual environments. How does this impact the culture?

Difficult to say, but multilingualism is certainly a feature of Sámi life. English is indeed becoming more widespread. Its use increased with the international organizing of indigenous peoples in the 1970s. And Norwegian and Swedish are very different from Finnish and Russian. Especially younger Sámi like to use English. Maybe Sámi and English will be the future, and the national languages will become less important.

Your academic field is literature. Is it possible to point to any specific characteristics of Sámi literature?

Cliché or not, the connection to the land is very central. It is crucial for our existence as indigenous people. Our creation myth defines us both as the children of the sun and the earth—in fact, the words for earth, mother, and river are all closely connected in the Sámi language: *eana, eadni, eatnu*. According to the myth, the heart of a two-year-old reindeer cow was put into the earth by the Great Creator. Whenever the Sámi feel threatened, they can listen to the earth, and if they still hear the heart of the reindeer cow beating, there is a future. The beating of the heart in the earth reverberates with that of our own heart.

And you find these features even in modern Sámi literature?
Yes. Obviously, Sámi literature undergoes changes, it has become very diverse, and there are modern varieties with many influences. But we find traditional motifs regularly. We also see parallels to the literature of other indigenous peoples.

I have asked others about the phenomenon of Sámi artists often engaging in several forms of artistic expression: visual art, music, poetry, and so forth. Synnøve Persen pointed out that Sámi always needed several legs to stand on in order to survive. What's your explanation?
I think it also has to do with our holistic view of the world. Aristotelian divisions don't make much sense in Sápmi. Nils-Aslak Valkeapää said that he found it impossible to view poetry just as language. Poetry has its own music. When he wrote poetry, he heard music, yoik, in the back of his head. It makes you look at the world differently, and it has an impact on how you express yourself artistically. This has survived centuries of colonialism. It impacts Sámi scholars, too. Most of us do more than one way of research.

What do you mean?
The first generation of Sámi scholars was brought up in very traditional academic ways. They did research according to the Western model. The next generation reflected on that and started to do things differently. Sámi values were included in their work. The first generation hadn't lost those values, but they kept them apart from their academic work. Israel Ruong, for example, was a classic academic on the one hand, and a Sámi politician on the other. Today, Sámi scholars do not make that distinction, and they do not strictly distinguish between art and scholarship either. This is true for indigenous scholarship in general. Many of my academic colleagues in North America are novelists and poets as well. I have written essays and plays and have worked as a journalist. There is a strong desire to make our work accessible to everyone in the community.

Is this where the concept of "decolonizing academia" comes in?
Linda Tuhiwai Smith's book *Decolonizing Methodologies*, published in 1999, was very important, and the focus on "indigenous methodologies" has opened many doors. But the problem with decolonization as a method is that the focus lies on colonization. Linda's husband Graham Hingangaroa Smith, also a scholar, has stressed the importance of "transformative action," where the focus lies on changing the situation and putting emphasis on your own language and worldview. This requires bringing your entire culture into research. Today, we use terms like "indigenism" and "transindigenous studies." Many are convinced that we need to get past "postcolonialism" and put more energy into conducting research on our own terms.

What's wrong with postcolonialism?
We are not past colonialism, and, in the case of the Sámi, we will likely never get there. To have our own independent country is an unrealistic goal. We will continue to be a minority within majority societies, but we want self-determination in culture, education, and other fields of life. I'm not sure why everyone is so afraid of that. We pose no threat for Western academia. We are very few. We won't replace it; we just want to add our own values and worldviews.

How important are the contacts with indigenous scholars from around the world for the development of Sámi scholarship?
They are crucial. We started connecting in the 1970s. The World Council of Indigenous Peoples provided a forum for indigenous peoples from all over the world to meet. Art and politics were always mixed. At our gatherings, there were political debates during the day and cultural activities in the evenings, and this really brought people together. The scholarship came as a result of that.

When I started to do academic work on Sámi literature, I knew I had to bring in the yoik, the storytelling tradition, and visual arts as well, because they tell their own stories. When I got more acquainted with Native American literature, I realized that the same approach was needed there. I met American Indian professors who told me they are able to express themselves better in fiction than in academic writing. I can relate to that, but it is also important to bring Sámi themes into academia.

A 1993 article of yours is called "The 'White Indians' of Scandinavia." Why that title?
That's what the Sámi often were called at the time. It had a self-ironic touch, as many other indigenous peoples were skeptical of our white faces.

Mari Boine told me about a conference in Germany where that skepticism only disappeared once she sang.
Nils-Aslak Valkeapää made the same experience at the founding congress of the World Council of Indigenous Peoples. Many delegates from Latin America were very skeptical of the Sámi. But when he performed a yoik, it went straight to their hearts. It's a great example of how art brings people together. And that's a major reason why I've been collaborating with artists so much. It makes connections to other indigenous people much easier. If you're the only Sámi in a nonindigenous academic delegation, this can be very hard. People just wonder why you're traveling with all these white guys.

You're the editor of a book called *Sami Culture in a New Era*, released in 1997. It seems groundbreaking to me, with great articles reflecting on Sámi life and identity in the late twentieth century. Was it a unique book at the time?
I think so. I wanted to do it in English because I felt there was a lack of Sámi perspectives in international debate. And we wanted to shed light on important topics that had long been neglected, such as health in Sámi communities.

When I read the book, I felt that much of it was still highly relevant.
Work done twenty years ago always seems old, but it might indeed remain more relevant than I think. After all, we're going through a process a recolonization rather than decolonization.

How so?
A very concrete example are the wind farms that are built all over Sápmi. We have no free space anymore, the colonizers have taken

so much. And it's not only the Sámi who get hurt, it's everyone living here. It's bad for the environment and for our peace of mind. We no longer have a haven.

You mentioned self-determination before, but also that a Sámi state is an unrealistic goal. What does self-determination mean without having your own state?
It's a complicated debate and conclusions are far off. Some people prefer to speak of "sovereignty," although that's often limited to culture. You could argue that doing scholarship in the Sámi language is an expression of sovereignty, but how far does that get you politically? The reality is that most Sámi today don't read the language. If we want to make a broader impact, we need to express ourselves in various ways.

To me, self-determination essentially means that we are doing things our own way. As a Sámi scholar, I don't feel the need to refer to all the important Western academics. I don't want to present their view; I want to present the Sámi view. Trusting your own people, your background, your ancestors, what they did, what they lived for, and what they believed in—that's the basis for self-determination. The question of whether we have our own state or not is really secondary. In fact, if we did, we'd very likely become dependent on multinational corporations. We have to face the changes in the world system. Nation-states are no longer as powerful as they once were. In the future, our biggest enemies might not be Oslo, Stockholm, and Helsinki, but multinationals trying to squeeze anything they can out of our territories.

There are examples of minorities in European nation-states with strong autonomy rights. I'm thinking of the German-speaking community in Italy, or the Swedish-speaking community in Finland. Are these models that could strengthen the political self-determination of Sápmi?
I've been thinking along similar lines. We often compare our situation exclusively to that of our indigenous brothers and sisters. We are in a better situation than most of them, and having our own parliaments seems like a big step. But there are autonomous regions in Europe whose inhabitants have much stronger rights than we do, and maybe we should be talking more about

that. Despite having our own parliaments, we remain fully in the pockets of the nation-state governments. They control the courts, allocate the money, and so on.

I think what we're dealing with is a common dynamic: our situation is not desperate and we've kind of settled into what we have, even if it is far from just. And we are overwhelmed with legal and bureaucratic hurdles forced upon us by the government. This is part of what Graham Hingangaroa Smith has called the "politics of distraction." It pushes the discussion about self-determination into the background, while it is crucial for our future.

What gives me hope is that people in the Western world begin to understand the importance of indigenous values: the connection to the land, the respect for nature and all its inhabitants. These values will be crucial if we want humankind to survive.

we were a wind

Nils-Aslak Valkeapää

This is poem no. 546 in Nils-Aslak Valkeapää, *The Sun, My Father*, translated by Harald Gaski, Lars Nordström, and Ralph Salisbury (Guovdageaidnu: DAT, 1997; original Sámi edition: *Beaivi, áhčážan* Guovdageaidnu: DAT, 1988). Reprinted with kind permission from the publisher and the Lásságámmi Foundation.

wind

we were a wind

life's singing wind

caressing the cheeks of the tundra

the forests, the valleys

a disappearing yoik

the reds of evening, wind

we were a wind

we came and left

and nothing remained of us

but a yoik in the singing wind

a dream about being

Aslak Holmberg

Photo: Kukka Ranta

Aslak Holmberg (born 1988) is a salmon fisher, Sámi language teacher, indigenous studies scholar, and vice president of the Sámi Council. He is active in various initiatives resisting colonial power and a prominent speaker on Sámi rights. I visited him at his family's home in Njuorggán, on the banks of the Deatnu River, in June 2019.

Since I don't speak Finnish, it's much harder for me to follow media coverage of Sámi issues in Finland than in Sweden and Norway. What am I missing?

Not much. Finnish media is very focused on conflict and scandal. This applies particularly to the Sámi. In the yellow press, the "angry Sámi" is a common feature. It's an image that's easy to sell, because the general public knows so little about the Sámi. You get away with belittling and ridiculing Sámi concerns. When the use of fake Sámi clothing by the tourist industry comes up, no one gets angry at the tourist industry; everyone just thinks the Sámi are oversensitive. Journalists also like to discuss who the "real" Sámi are, usually without speaking to any Sámi.

Things have changed a little in recent years. The Deatnu River protests have gotten a fair bit of attention and caused more serious debate.

Can you tell us about the protests?

In 2017, the governments of Finland and Norway passed new fishing regulations for the Deatnu River, which, including tributaries, marks the border between Finland and Norway for more than two hundred kilometers. Sámi live on both sides of the river, and they've been fishing salmon in it for centuries. The new regulations affect primarily our traditional ways of fishing.

I know very little about fishing. Can you explain?

The Deatnu River is one of the very few salmon rivers where you can fish with nets. That's what we do. But rod fishing has higher status. If you look at the new regulations, there is only one very specific group of fishers that gains something: the Finnish cabin owners who have bought property along the river with fishing rights attached to it. It's all about lobbying power.

What's the official explanation for the new regulations?

They are supposed to protect the salmon. But essentially they are just shifting fishing rights from one group, the Sámi, to another, the cabin owners. The consequences go far beyond fishing. Our entire culture is based on the fishing tradition, so when our fishing rights are restricted, our entire culture is under threat.

A prominent actor in the protests is the group Ellos Deatnu! What does it mean in English?
"Let Deatnu live!" or, as we've translated it in our documents, "Long live Deatnu!" Deatnu is the Sámi name for both the river and the valley.

Once the new regulations were passed, you occupied an island on the river.
Well, we don't like to call it an occupation, because you can't really occupy something that's yours.

Good point. You set up a camp on one of the islands.
Yes, and we called for a moratorium. Basically, we established an area where the new fishing regulations would not be followed, arguing that they lacked any approval by the Sámi rights holders.

We stayed on the island during the whole summer of 2017. In 2018, we set up camp again but didn't stay as long. Our signs are up again this summer: "Fishing only with the permission of local families." The moratorium is still in place.

How did the authorities react?
We wrote letters to the relevant ministries in both Finland and Norway, questioning their authority in the matter and informing them about the moratorium. The only response we got was from the Finnish minister for agriculture and forestry, who said that the regulations were passed in accordance with the law and that we had to abide by them.

And that was it?
That was it.

No police ever came to the island?
Apparently, Norwegian authorities had asked the Finnmark police to intervene, as the island lies on the Norwegian side. But no one ever showed up.

You said you questioned the authority of the governments to regulate fishing along the Deatnu River. Is that because of ethical

principle, or do the regulations also violate rights of the Sámi that the governments have actually granted them?

A big problem for us is that much of this is unclear. The governments recognize us as indigenous people, which means that our way of life ought to be protected and that we ought to be involved in making the decisions that affect our way of life. But how that translates into legislation is open to interpretation. For the Finnish government, for example, it is enough to invite us to a hearing and let us voice our concerns—then, the politicians and officials go off and make their own decisions. Obviously, that's not how I interpret it. It's a far cry from anything that could reasonably be seen as respecting the right to self-determination. In the case of the new fishing regulations, all of the Sámi who went to the government hearings were against them. It made no difference.

You said that the Deatnu protests did influence public debate on Sámi rights in Finland. How influential was the Suohpanterror collective?

Suohpanterror addresses Sámi issues throughout Sápmi, but its influence might have been biggest in Finland, with their art being featured in big exhibitions in Helsinki and the like. The collective has certainly helped raise awareness about the Sámi and our situation.

You mentioned cultural exploitation by the tourist industry. Tourism has become an important economic factor along the Deatnu River as well. How does that impact the Sámi community?

Tourism has become the biggest industry here. During the summer, the population doubles. Local Sámi already expressed concern during the first tourist boom, in the 1950s. Today, there are ten times as many tourists. In 2016, more than thirty thousand daily fishing licenses were sold. Obviously, that has an impact on Sámi fishing, but it has also generated new sources of income, at least on the Finnish side, where most of the tourists are. Here, the interests of the locals and the tourists partly overlap. Most tourists were also hurt by the new fishing regulations. As I said, it was a very specific group that benefited.

Cultural exploitation is not a huge concern in the Deatnu Valley. Sámi are a majority here and run most of the tourist enterprises. It is a bigger concern farther south, in tourist centers like Roavvenjárga and Levi.

In an interview, I heard you make a distinction between "cultural" and "political" nationalism. Can you explain?
The goal of political nationalism is to establish a state for the nation. I see that as an absurd goal for the Sámi. We are a minority almost everywhere we live. Cultural nationalism, on the other hand, emphasizes the specific characteristics of one's own culture in distinction from other cultures. It doesn't mean to be separated from them. We live alongside other cultures all across Sápmi. We have no interest in drawing borders. All we want is a form of coexistence in which our culture is respected. Today, this is not the case. The governments of the states occupying Sápmi have always acted as if they have the right to dominate everyone. I see cultural nationalism as a protection against this.

The term "nation" is often highly contested. What is the word you use in Sámi?
In Sámi, we speak of *álbmot*, which is closer to "people." When I say "nation" in English, I use it more or less as a synonym. *Álbmot* is also close to *olbmot*, which means "human beings."

I'm asking because I feel the use of the term "nation" can sometimes confuse people, as it has two rather different meanings: it can relate to a "people," the way you describe it, and it can relate to a nation-state, which you might be a citizen of, but which doesn't define your culture. It seems that the political Right is sometimes conflating these two meanings for their political purposes.
Being a "Finn" is a construct that was needed to build a national identity when Finland was fighting for independence. Even the Sámi were incorporated into this identity as "one of the Finnish tribes." But Sámi culture has nothing to do with Finland. It doesn't change when you cross the border to Norway. The same is true for Karelians: it doesn't matter whether you live in Finland or Russia, you are still Karelian.

At the same time, it is true that I hold a Finnish passport, and there is no denying that the Sámi living on the Finnish side of Sápmi have been influenced by living here: we live under Finnish laws, we go to Finnish schools, we learn the Finnish language. There are differences between me and my family on the other side of the river, because we've been separated by colonial borders. But that doesn't make me a "Finnish person." I'm a Sámi person.

Having said that, people interpret their identities differently. I just met a man on the Swedish side who told me that he was "100 percent Sámi and 100 percent Swedish." I know that you find Sámi on the Finnish side who say similar things. But I can't look past the history of assimilation and the attempts by the colonial governments to erase our identity. Maybe I'd feel different if our relationship to the Finnish state was different. But it is an unhealthy relationship. Finland is not my country and it doesn't represent my people's way of life.

In 2017, Finland celebrated 100 years of independence. You released a short animated film titled *Finland's 100 Years of Colonialism*. Can you tell us about it?

The idea came from the Michael Moore movie *Bowling for Columbine*. It includes a short animated clip of a few minutes about the history of the United States. Now, everything that needs to be boiled down to five minutes will be a bit of a caricature, but I thought something similar could be done for Finland. I was so tired of hearing how great everything had been since independence—especially when the new fishing laws had just turned me into a criminal in my own home. I wanted to do something to spoil the party at least a little bit.

One evening, I was lying in my bed unable to go to sleep, and I suddenly realized that the deadline for the application to the Sámi Council's cultural funds was about to run out. I checked my watch and saw that I had twenty minutes left. Luckily, I only had to fill out an online form with ten questions and add a work schedule and a budget. I managed to send it off in time. A few weeks later, I got the funds I needed to do the film. I found a Sámi animator, Jouni West, who lives two hours upstream, and he did a great job.

So, you provided him with the script, and he did all the graphics?

Yes, but I sent pretty clear guidelines. Nonetheless, he added his own touch. I never intended the person on stage to look like me. But that's fine.

In 2018, you won an award at the University of Tromsø for your master's thesis, "Bivdit Luosa—To Ask for Salmon: Traditional Knowledge on Salmon and the River Deatnu." In your acceptance speech, you stressed the importance for people to study their own communities. What makes this so important?

Knowledge is power, and it is used to serve certain interests. With respect to indigenous people, this often means that the colonizers come, claim to have all the knowledge, and do whatever serves their own interests. To deny that indigenous people have knowledge is a justification for denying them control over their lives. But we know how things work where we live, and control over our lives should be left to us.

In my thesis, I was looking at different forms of knowledge, and I discussed what knowledge means among the Sámi. It's more complicated than a biologist showing you some numbers. There is always a subjective element in research, and there are always things you know nothing about. Culture plays an important role.

I'd like see more indigenous people engage in this debate, not least the youth. Who comes to study your community? Do these people really know anything about it? When people come from the outside, why do they come? What are their interests? Often enough, it's just to advance their academic careers. When we study our own communities, it's much more likely that we actually want to help them.

I have also heard you say that while the colonial cultures might be gone in a thousand years from now, the Sámi will still be here. Was that for provocation or do you really think that to be true?

It was something a friend said to me, and I thought it was put very well. We often interpret struggle in negative ways: it's about what you oppose or need to be protected from. But our history of struggle has taught us a lot. We know what we as a people can do and what we cannot do. We have learned to be survivors. We are used to struggling against the forces of globalization. Majority cultures, which are not as strongly rooted in tradition, are much more prone to be erased by them. Consumerism turns everything into one big blur. We are better prepared for the future.

Moratorium in Čearretsuolu

Ellos Deatnu!

Taken from www.ellosdeatnu.wordpress.com.

A Moratorium is declared in the area of Čearretsuolu island regarding the new fishing regulations for the Deatnu (Tana/Teno) River, as the new regulations threaten the well-being of the Saami from the Deatnu Valley. Salmon fishing plays an indispensable part in the Saami way of life. The new regulations represent a clear violation of human and indigenous rights as well as of the constitutions of Norway and Finland, and these were negotiated with negligible consultation of the local Saami community. A Moratorium means that the implementation of the new fishing regulations is halted in the area surrounding Čearretsuolu. Čearretsuolu with its surrounding area is Saami territory.

Fishing in the Moratorium area may not in any way hamper Saami fishing rights or interests. These rights are firmly rooted in the conventions, declarations and recommendations of international law. They are also supported by Norwegian and Finnish state constitutions, Saami concepts of justice and Saami customary law.

This Moratorium is in force until new regulations are negotiated for fishing in the Deatnu. These new fishing regulations are to be negotiated in a proper and fair way using Free, Prior and Informed Consent, and all discussions are to be led by local Saami people. During the Moratorium in this region, Saami concepts of justice and Saami customary law will be applied.

Since the newly imposed regulations are halted, any tourist fishing licenses that are not locally approved will not be in force in this region. Tourist fishers must therefore ask permission from the Saami people of the Deatnu Valley, and especially from the family whose traditional area this is, i.e. the Helándirs.

We encourage people in the Deatnu Valley to declare a Moratorium in other areas along the Deatnu watershed as well until new fishing regulations have been negotiated and implemented.

Ellos Deatnu!—Long live Deatnu!

June 21, 2017

Stefan Mikaelsson

Photo courtesy of Stefan Mikaelsson

Stefan Mikaelsson (born 1957) is a reindeer herder and longtime Sámi politician. He was chairman of the Sámi Parliament in Sweden from 2009 to 2017. In the 2018 Swedish Parliament elections, he ran for the Feminist Initiative. A staunch defender of Sámi rights, Stefan is a highly respected figure among Sámi activists long beyond the confines of party politics. We had tea and coffee in Suttes in June 2019.

You are just coming from calf marking. It is an important event in reindeer herding and Sámi culture. What happens?
Each spring, the cows are calving, and in the summer you collect the herd and mark the calves' ears. This takes a few days. You see how the past year has been for the herd, how many animals you have lost, and how many of the calves have made it. Many fall victim to predators, and others survive. The marking of the calves presents you with the results of one year's work.

The marks that are used run in the family?
Naturally, yes, although there might be slight variations between relatives. But the owner of the reindeer can be identified by the particular mark they cut.

You are a reindeer owner and belong to a sameby. In Sweden, people often stress the division between Sámi reindeer owners and other Sámi. Is this exaggerated by the media or is it a problem you also had to deal with as a Sámi politician?
It is a problem, but a problem that has been created by the Swedish state. The government wanted to limit the number of Sámi, and one way to do this was to exclude everyone who didn't own reindeer. The division is enshrined in Swedish law. The same law discriminates against Sámi women, for whom it is very difficult to gain membership in a sameby.

Is it different in the other states occupying Sápmi?
Yes. In Norway, where the majority of the Sámi live, this conflict doesn't exist. In Norway, Sámi are Sámi, no matter whether they own reindeer or not. Not all Sámi can or want to own reindeer. Nonetheless, in Sweden, your identity as a Sámi is questioned if you don't. This has a long history, and it's difficult to get away from it. The state's strategy has been very successful.

I discussed the case of Jovsset Ánte Sara with Øyvind Ravna. Is forced culling of reindeer a big problem in Sweden, too?
It has been, but it's not so common these days. In the 1930s, the government ordered seven thousand reindeer to be slaughtered near Árjepluovve. That's a lot. It's ironic that the government has often justified the forced culling with reindeer moving into a certain

area "illegally." But it's only the government that has made this illegal.

Aren't arguments about protecting the environment used as well?
The Sámi have protected their environment successfully for a very long time. We know when an area is overpopulated and how to solve the problem. It doesn't need anyone else to make that decision. Besides, reindeer herding is far less damaging to the environment than most other forms of husbandry or agriculture.

You've had a long career as a Sámi politician. How did it begin?
Sture Nilsson, who founded *Skogssamerna*, the "Forest Sámi Party," in 1993, was my mentor. It was a natural step to get involved. I remember the happiness during the first session of the Sámi Parliament: to have reindeer owners and other Sámi, men and women, come together on equal footing. It is often said that the Sámi Parliament has no political power and that things are moving too slowly, but there have been achievements, too. In 2013, we strongly condemned the plans for establishing a mine in Gállok. A few months later, the local authorities objected to the plans as well. There is no alternative to the Sámi Parliament. Sámi organizations don't have the same reach and influence.

It's interesting to hear you say that, because in the 2013 book *Queering Sápmi* you state, "The Sámi Parliament is a disaster."
Well, you can state many things. What I was referring to was my first term as chairman. That was really a low point in the parliament's history. We had four boards in four years, and the administrative chaos made political work very difficult. But things have improved again.

You were also a member of the Sámi Council. How do you see the relationship between the Sámi Council and the Sámi parliaments?
I think they complement each other well. They also collaborate in pushing certain demands, for example the one for a Sámi bureau at the European Union in Brussels. This would be an important step.

How about the Swedish government ratifying the ILO Convention 169?

Of course that would be an important step, too. The Sámi Parliament in Sweden has urged the government to do so about ten times. The last time was two years ago, and there wasn't even a debate. There is a clear consensus on the issue among the parliament's members.

At a Sámi Parliament session in Tråante in 2017, you quoted Elsa Laula: "I have tried to organize the Sámi as a people. But it didn't work." Why did you choose that quote?
We were in Tråante to celebrate the one-hundredth anniversary of the 1917 Sámi National Assembly that Elsa Laula had organized. The quote is from an interview she gave in 1929. I felt it was relevant, as it illustrates both her vision and her disappointment. The Sámi were recognized as a nation in the Strömstadt Treaty of 1751, but for many Sámi, including Elsa Laula, it was difficult to see them united as a nation due to hundreds of years of colonialism.

Do you find it important to speak of a "Sámi nation"?
Yes, very important. I try to do this as often as I can.

Why?
We have everything that is usually attributed to a nation: our own language, culture, and tradition. They were created by ourselves and existed long before the nation-states were created. Their leaders drew borders because they couldn't unite. We never needed borders.

So a nation does not need a state?
No, not necessarily. The Sámi don't need a state. We can have a Sámi region that includes parts of Norway, Sweden, Finland, and Russia. If you have your own state, you need a police force, a foreign office, maybe an army. I'm not sure that any of this would help us.

Speaking about armies: at a speech about the planned mine in Gállok, you pointed out the connections between mining and militarism. I thought that was very interesting, because the issue isn't raised much. People mainly talk about the environmental consequences of mining.
It's the conclusion I have come to. If you look at the areas that are used for mining, they are also the areas used for military training

and weapons testing. And if we take the example of Sweden, we're not just talking about the Swedish Army. There are also other powers flying their drones over Sámi settlements.

One more quote from your Tråante speech: "There is good reason to say that Swedish parliamentarism is rooted in racism." What do you mean?

In 1922, the State Institute for Racial Biology in Uppsala was established, based on a motion passed in the Swedish Parliament. The institute existed until 1958. Some people downplay that history, saying that research there effectively ended in the 1930s. But later this year, we will meet in Liksjoe to receive twenty-five Sámi skeletons. In other words, Sámi skeletons remain in Swedish institutions to this day. How is this not a continuation of racial biology? The Sámi Parliament demanded all skeletons to be returned years ago.

In Sweden, the parties in the Sámi Parliament mainly represent different interest groups, from Forest Sámi to reindeer herders. In Norway, the parties are more ideologically oriented. What's better?

I'm happy with the way it is in Sweden. In Norway, most of the mainstream political parties have representatives in the Sámi Parliament. I don't think having the parties of the Swedish Parliament represented in the Sámi Parliament would help us. They have never done anything for the Sámi—or, for that matter, anyone living in the remote areas of the country.

Before the last parliamentary elections in Sweden, you were a candidate for the Feminist Initiative. I assume that means you don't see it like the other parties.

The Feminist Initiative has a clear indigenous profile and there were several indigenous people on their list. This is also reflected in their understanding of feminism. Indigenous feminism is not the same as European feminism or the feminism advocated by the Swedish government.

What's the difference?

Gender inequality affects indigenous women in particular ways, because they are already denied their rights as indigenous people.

For indigenous women, access to land and water is central. That's not on the agenda of European feminists.

In 2012, you described yourself as queer on Sámi radio. This got much attention in Swedish media. Had it been the same if you were not Sámi?
Probably not. But I was also chairman of the Sámi Parliament at the time, which made it particularly interesting, I suppose. It's not a big deal for Swedish men to break gender norms, but Sámi society is seen as conservative and unable to change.

I've heard people say that there was no machismo in traditional Sámi society, but that it developed with colonialism.
I see it that way, too. As Sámi men, we have adopted attitudes that help us survive in majority culture. We've become very insecure with regard to our own traditions, and this includes more modest and gentler forms of masculinity.

Do you feel it was good that you instigated a debate about gender roles?
Yes. I didn't expect that much attention, but I felt I could use it to influence young Sámi men in a positive way. It was certainly more effective than a decision made at a plenary session in parliament.

At the first Sápmi Pride in Giron in 2014, you stood next to young Sámi activists, raising your fist during the opening ceremony. In the political world I come from, there is a fairly strict distinction between activists on the street and politicians in their offices. This distinction doesn't seem to exist in Sápmi in the same way. Is that true?
Yes, it's very different. Of course I join young activists who do important work for Sámi culture. It's also important to show that we can take such initiatives ourselves and we don't need anyone else to do it for us. Sweden's political parties have a very different agenda.

Which is?
To come to power, to hold on to it, to impose your own ideas on anyone else, and to make profit, no matter the consequences. The

Sámi have paid dearly for this. They have lost their land and they had to fight very hard not to lose their culture as well.

I heard you say that you were thinking about writing a "Sámi Manifesto" once you retire from politics. Is this still the plan?
I'd like to write a book. I have much to tell. And we have to instill pride and strength in our youth, who still have to struggle for true self-determination. I got the idea when I read that Winston Churchill had plans to retreat to the Reid's Palace Hotel on Madeira to write his memoirs. It doesn't have to be the Reid's Palace, but Madeira would be nice.

The Sámi Parliament in Sweden Cannot Accept the Exploitation of Sápmi

The following statement by the Sámi Parliament in Sweden was read out in Gállok on August 28, 2013. It had been adopted unanimously in a plenary session the day before. Translated by G.K. from the Swedish version published on www.sametinget.se.

In connection with the ongoing exploitation of Sápmi by mining enterprises—including the test drillings in Gállok near Jåhkåmåhke and the plans for a mine in Raavrhjohke near Dearna, which are obvious breaches of the Sámi's human rights as well as their rights as indigenous people to control their own culture, land, and environment—the Sámi Parliament in Sweden demands . . .

- that the Swedish state stops all prospecting and test drilling, and does not issue mining concessions, until it is ensured that Sweden respects the international agreements on the rights of indigenous people, especially the principles of "Free, Prior, and Informed Consent," which need to guide all decisions that affect the Sámi people.
- that the Sámi Parliament is granted actual power over Sámi land.
- that legislation will be changed in a way that prioritizes the Sámi's need to access unpolluted land and water over the profit interests of foreign venture capitalists.
- that national interests are reevaluated in ways that prioritize long-term interests over short-term profits.
- that sustainable environments are of the highest priority, enabling current and future generations to maintain their culture, ensure physical and mental health, and practice traditional livelihoods.
- that the environment necessary for Sámi livelihoods such as reindeer herding, hunting, fishing, *duodji*, tourism, and others to flourish must not be threatened by short-sighted exploitation, and that the right to reindeer herding protected in the Constitution is respected.

- that cultural and psycho-social consequences must be considered in all political decisions concerning Sápmi.

According to the Swedish Constitution, the Sámi are an indigenous people with internationally recognized rights. In the United Nations, countries work together to ensure that the rights of indigenous peoples to their land and culture are protected. Already in the International Covenant on Civil and Political Rights of 1966, the peoples of the world are granted the right to self-determination. This has since been emphasized in international agreements on indigenous rights. Conventions have been added to strengthen the rights of children, women, workers, and other vulnerable social groups. The rights of indigenous people to their land and culture as well as social development have been laid out in the 1989 International Labour Organization Convention 169 and the 2007 United Nations Declaration on the Rights of Indigenous Peoples as well as in the Convention on Biological Diversity, signed in 1992, and various other international conventions, declarations, and resolutions.

We find it deplorable that the state's mineral strategy and its review of mineral laws contradicts the government's promise to protect the traditional livelihoods of the Arctic. The mineral policy that Sweden is practicing today stands for a continued colonization of Sápmi and the Sámi people.

The Sámi Parliament cannot accept the ongoing exploitation of Sápmi. The Sámi Parliament will continue to work for sustainable forms of development that guarantee all Sámi the possibility to live and work in Sápmi.

May-Britt Öhman

Photo courtesy of May-Britt Öhman

May-Britt Öhman (born 1966) is a researcher who holds a PhD in the history of technology. Currently, she works at the Centre for Multidisciplinary Studies on Racism (CEMFOR) at Uppsala University and at Luleå University of Technology. She has organized several conferences to strengthen Sámi and indigenous perspectives in research and education and champions a "Sámiland Free University." Find out more about May-Britt's activities at www.maybrittohman.com. We talked via video stream in July 2019.

You have written that, as a Sámi scholar, you have to deal with "a colonial situation both within academia and outside." Can you elaborate?
It's a very long list—I don't even know where to begin. But let's look at my work in academia. I don't have tenure. I know that it has become harder to get tenure for everyone, but the topics I work on, and the way I work, have not been beneficial for an academic career. I regularly help others with their work without taking credit for it. I feel it's important to give them a platform, but from a career perspective, it means that I'm "losing" articles. If my approach was different, I might find myself in a different position now.

It is difficult to work in a Sámi way within academia. It's not part of Sámi culture to take other people's words and present them as your own, but this is what much of academia relies on. Furthermore, knowledge about Sámi culture is close to nonexistent. You can become a university professor, even in history, without ever having learned anything about it. If you look at the way science, engineering, and economics are taught, it is all about the exploitation of resources and the domination of nature. It's all very colonial.

And outside of academia? What would be an example?
The fact that we speak Swedish right now, and that I have never learned to speak Sámi. That's a very obvious one. And then there are all the consequences of colonial policies: mining, dams, clearcuts—all of which undermine Sámi culture. We aren't talking about abstract concepts here. The foundations of Sámi culture have been under threat for centuries. This is very real.

Some people would argue that the interest in Sámi culture has increased, or that Sámi are more visible in the media. Would you disagree with that?
There is no contradiction. The media—and, for that matter, the politicians—like to speak fondly of the Sámi and their beautiful clothes, their exotic way of life, and so on. All the while, the material conditions for maintaining their way of life are erased.

You don't make a distinction between being an academic and an activist. Some people think it's hard to have one foot in the university and the other outside. Have you found this to be difficult?

This is all based on the assumption that research is not political. But it is. This starts with the questions you ask. The problem is a different one: as soon as you point out the political dimensions of research, people will use this against you.

What do you mean?
It's convenient for those in power to pretend that research is not political, so they can discredit their opponents' work as being politically motivated. But all of academia is political.

I guess there is also the critique of academic theory not being of practical relevance.
I think that critique comes from people who don't like what you do. No one who shares my feminist and indigenous perspectives has ever voiced any such criticism. People who aren't in academia find it encouraging that there is research that supports what they are saying. I don't think it matters so much how you say it. The biggest problem with academia is that whole communities remain excluded. The Sámi have long been nothing but a topic of academic research; they have not been involved themselves. It's not about theory or practice, it's about participation.

Hasn't there been significant change in the last twenty years with Sámi research programs being established and more Sámi scholars entering academia?
When I entered academia in the early 1990s, there wasn't a single Sámi academic I knew. Yes, this has changed. In Sweden, there are now Sámi research programs in Ubmeje and Uppsala, and such programs exist in Norway and Finland as well. People turn to Sámi scholars for advice, we get invited to lectures, and so on. But there still are researchers who aren't Sámi studying Sámi communities without giving anything back.

You developed a vision of what you call the "Sámiland Free University." Can you tell us about that?
It's very hard to get funding for Sámi research. The Sámi institutions have limited resources, and if you go elsewhere there's a lack of knowledge. Let's say you apply for European Union funds. Where do you find reviewers who know anything about the Sámi?

I call this "knowledge colonialism." We need to strengthen the production of indigenous knowledge instead. The Sámiland Free University is my challenge to the colonial production of knowledge in Sweden. I'll soon be fifty-three years old, and it's no realistic goal for me to establish an actual university, but I put the idea out there as a base to build on and to strengthen my own thinking. How would I act, write, talk if I was working at this Sámiland Free University? It is both empowering and challenging to reflect on this.

The entire educational system, as it is, implies the destruction of Sámi culture. It's demanding and tiring to fight this all the time. Sometimes, you can't even raise the issue that Sámi scholars need extra support without this being construed as "racism" toward other scholars. That's the level of debate we have to deal with. I've been asked by colleagues in the US why I don't go there and work under better conditions. But I don't want to leave; I want to build something here.

How strong are your connections to scholars in the US?
I have been collaborating with scholars in the US through international academic associations since I became a PhD student in 1999. However, I did not meet indigenous scholars until 2011, when I attended a conference of the Native American and Indigenous Studies Association. Kim TallBear, whom I had gotten in touch with through Sandra Harding, had told me about it. It was thrilling to meet so many indigenous scholars. Today, my connections to scholars in the US and Canada, both indigenous and nonindigenous, are very strong. Also to scholars in Australia, New Zealand/ Aotearoa, and Japan. I feel I belong to a network of very inspiring people. There is plenty of exchange and collaboration.

The following year you organized an international conference for indigenous scholars and activists in Uppsala.
"RE:Mindings," yes. We already had a gathering in 2011, and then in 2013 as well. All events were open to nonindigenous scholars and activists, too.

There is an extensive reader documenting the 2012 conference. A number of contributions address the situation in Gállok, where

people were protesting test drillings and the plans to establish a mine.

The reader has several articles on Gállok. In 2013, I founded a "Technoscience Research Group," and we organized a five-day workshop in Gállok in July, near the protest camp. In October 2013, we organized a conference at Uppsala University titled "Re:Claimings." It also included several presentations about Gállok with scholars, activists, and artists. Unfortunately, there is no documentation. I was simply too exhausted to get that organized. Academic publishing can be painful work.

What was the workshop in Gállok about?

Various things, from the impact of mining on groundwater and dam safety to herbal medicine and bow making.

What were your impressions from the protest camp?

It was inspiring to meet the activists, but being there was also unpleasant and scary in many ways. I had been active in a Facebook group where the mining plans were discussed, and I was pretty much the only one expressing concerns, especially with regard to dam safety. People in favor of the mine were very angry, and when I got invited to speak at an event in Jåhkåmåhke, there were protests. The venue was on top of a hill. Someone placed a huge rock on the road leading to it with a tractor. My mother came from Jåhkåmåhke, so my family knows the town well, and my brother was very concerned. The atmosphere was very aggressive. At the camp, the police were very violent in their attempts to clear it.

It has been claimed by some observers that there were few Sámi in the camp, I guess partly to suggest that the protesters didn't have as much support from the Sámi community as they claimed.

That's a very shortsighted interpretation. To begin with, reindeer herders are with their reindeer during the summer, so they couldn't be there. Other local Sámi regularly came to the camp, but there was no need for them to stay overnight. Many of the people who stayed their full-time were activists who had come from farther afield, but that doesn't mean there was no Sámi support. There was even an official delegation from the Sámi Parliament who came and declared their opposition to the mine.

Another thing that must not be forgotten is that local Sámi took a much bigger risk in getting involved than outside activists. As I said, the atmosphere was very aggressive. If you lived in the area, you had to fear repercussions that were very different from those for people who had no or little personal connection to the community. I was advised to keep a low profile while I was there.

You didn't know about your Sámi background before you were an adult. This is not an unusual story, it seems.

I have recently written two articles about what happened to my family during the nineteenth century. My grandfather's grandmother had a Sámi name and owned reindeer. She has often been described as the last "real Sámi" in my family. She and her sister made homes in the same area, with the difference that she was married to a man who was registered as a Swede, and her sister to a man who was registered as a Sámi. In the 1870s, parts of the land they were living on were confiscated by the state, a common practice. My grandfather's grandmother and her family were allowed to keep their home because they were registered as Swedes due to her husband. Her sister, whose family was registered as Sámi, lost everything. This is a very concrete example of how the reality of colonialism forced people to change their identities—and of the price paid by the people who didn't. If you wanted to be a reindeer herder and stick to your traditions, the Swedish state made it very hard. This was especially true for Forest Sámi, which my family were. Mountain Sámi were as oppressed but upheld as the bearers of reindeer herding. It's a classic example of divide and conquer. Many of us have been forced to deny and forget our Sámi heritage.

Once you knew about your family's history, did you embrace Sámi identity right away? I imagine this to be confusing on a personal level.

I was excited about what I had learned about my family, but no, I didn't embrace Sámi identity right away. I needed encouragement from others. Agneta Silversparf, who has helped many Sámi to reconnect with their family's past, was very important. In 2008, she invited me to attend a meeting of Vuovdega, one of the parties represented in Sweden's Sámi Parliament, and she also sewed my first traditional Sámi dress. I wore it at a research conference for the first time in 2011. At first, I felt a little awkward, but once again, I had the encouragement from others. I'm tremendously thankful for that.

You have a background in political science. I've been discussing the notion of Sámi self-determination in other interviews. How do you interpret it?

It's difficult to outline self-determination when you're dealing with hundreds of years of colonialism. Personally, I think it's worth looking at the world heritage site of Laponia and the involvement of the area's Sámi reindeer herders in administering it. At the center of Sámi self-determination must be the recognition of the Sámi's relationship to the land and natural resources, which is so different from those of Europeans and their money-driven system. Everyone would benefit from this. The traditional Sámi way of life is sustainable, and while we cannot return to the past, we can use our knowledge about the past to head into a better future.

Guidelines for a Sámiland Free University

May-Britt Öhman

Taken from the website www.samelandsfriauniversitet.com. Translated from Swedish by G.K.

- The majority of the research and teaching staff will be Sámi. Other scholars are welcome, but Sámi leadership is of crucial importance. It is also mandatory to have the diversity of Sámi languages, cultures, traditions, and backgrounds represented.
- According to Sámi tradition, any sense of belonging is inclusive. We reject the colonial categories created by racial biology and racism, which have caused conflict and partition.
- We analyze, discuss, and confront the traumas created by colonization.
- We regard Sámi knowledge as having as much value as academic knowledge, and sometimes as being more relevant.
- Science and knowledge are based on a holistic worldview; they always need to be critical.
- Knowledge and experience are created in different environments and are dependent on specific traditions and physical conditions. Our work is not reduced to one place ("campus") but to various places.
- A gender perspective and a commitment to equality and justice is mandatory for our work. Queer perspectives are of crucial importance, as are the perspectives of all oppressed or marginalized groups. The prohibited grounds of discrimination in Swedish law may serve as a guideline.
- All aspects of Sámi and indigenous life are of importance for scientific work, and they help to "create knowledge"—a literal translation of the Swedish word for science, *vetenskap*.
- We invite indigenous scholars—as well as scholars who are allies to indigenous peoples—from around the world to work with us.

- We aim for a respectful and fruitful exchange with "Western" society and its traditions of knowledge.
- We emphasize perspectives of power as well as conflicts within Sámi society; we analyze how Sámi can overcome these conflicts, and how we can make Sámi society better for everyone, regardless of which group they belong to, how they are categorized, or what their history is.
- We put a particular emphasis on neglected Sámi traditions and cultures.
- We aim to establish fruitful exchange with Swedish universities, places of higher learning, and decision-makers on all levels.
- Like any other university, we are independent of political parties; our work is rooted in human rights, democracy, and decolonization.
- It is of crucial importance to protect and strengthen the Sámi languages as well as Sámi values and forms of cultural expression.

Suvi West

Photo: Sanna Lehto

Suvi West (born 1982) is a filmmaker, TV worker, and storyteller. Her documentary films have screened at numerous festivals, and the comedy series *Njuoska bittut/Märät säpikkäät* (2012–2013) broke new ground in Sámi and Finnish television. Suvi is part of the Miracle Workers Collective, which represented Finland at the 2019 Venice Biennale, and of Siidaskuvla, a project aiming to decolonize Sámi society through reclaiming and reengaging with the traditional *siida* system. You can follow her on Instagram: @suviwest. We met in Gáregasnjárga in June 2019.

Can I ask you about some of the documentaries you have done?
Eh, okay.

Not really?
No, no, it's okay. It's just that once I get a project out of my system, I have a hard time even remembering it. But please go ahead and ask.

You made a documentary film about your grandfather who was a passenger in a plane that disappeared.
Yes, this was about forty years ago. My grandfather, Jouni Vest, was a Sámi politician and a member of the first Sámi Parliament, which was established in Finland in 1973. Together with other Sámi politicians, he was on his way to a conference in Snåase, on the Norwegian side of Sápmi, when their small plane disappeared near Bådåddjo.

And it was never found?
No. This had serious consequences for Sámi politics, because these were the people who had well-established contacts with the Finnish government. So it was a big thing politically, not just personally. But the film focuses more on the personal aspects. I tried to portray my grandfather, search for my relationship to him, and show how the grief affected my family. I also tried to find out more about what happened to the plane.

I assume there were different theories.
There was a lot of speculation. Everything from the governments of the Nordic countries being involved to the plane having been captured by the Soviets. However, after much research and reflection, I think it was an accident. The plane probably lies at the bottom of the ocean.

Are more people in your family politically active?
I have a cousin, Sandra Márjá West, who is in the Sámi Parliament on the Norwegian side. In general, though, we are better known for our artistic practices. My extended family includes everything from writers and filmmakers to visual artists and singers. We are politically active through our creative work.

You've done other films with personal topics. *Me and My Little Sister* focuses on the relationship to your sister Kaisa. What is it about?
I'm still trying to figure that out. I think it's about the journey of two sisters, where one tries to protect the other and eventually finds out that that's not her job. The background is being queer in Finland and Sápmi. It's often interpreted as a Sámi film, but to me it's not. I don't even see it as a queer film. It's a film about sisterhood.

You also did a documentary titled *On the Edge of Life*, about people taking their own.
It is one of the films I was asked to do. Suicide rates are very high in the Arctic region, and they are particularly high among indigenous peoples.

And you were looking at the reasons?
Yes. It's very complex. If you look at the statistics, they are times when the rates are particularly high. A specific event can trigger a wave of suicides, and there might be an element of emulating others. But even at other times, it's become a common way of dealing with personal problems. The wounds of colonialism are a big part of it. The indigenous cultures of the Arctic region have all been exposed to strict assimilation policies, and it can be very difficult to be an indigenous person not raised in indigenous ways. It makes you question your identity and creates a heavy burden for many of us. A current factor is also hate speech, especially online. Minorities, including Sámi, are strongly affected by it.

You've done documentaries about painful issues like this one, but what made you most famous was a comedy series, is that right?
Yes, and it's probably what I will always be best known for, at least in Finland.

The program was called *Njuoska bittut* in North Sámi, or *Märät säpik-käät* in Finnish. The only English translation I've ever seen was "Wet Reindeer Fur Leggings." It was marketed as a Sámi comedy show. You and Kirste Aikio wrote, directed, and starred in it. The show ran for two seasons, 2012–2013. What kinds of reactions did you get?
Lots of different ones. Plenty of critique, plenty of love, and everything in between. It was a very unique show for Finland, we didn't

follow any established pattern. I think it confused a lot of people, and many thought the show was just weird.

There were two Finnish characters who appeared regularly: a pair of drunk women with bad teeth sitting on the curb, complaining about everything under the sun. Were you never criticized for stereotyping?
No. I love those characters. But you need to understand the Finnish context to appreciate that. There was a duo of Finnish comedians in the 1980s that was very popular. Among their characters were two Sámi who had hair made of hay, wore odd clothes, and were always drunk. They sang a silly song, a parody of a yoik, which every Sámi in Finland has been forced to listen to hundreds of times. If people find out you are Sámi, you get to hear it to this day, especially in bars. This is what we were referencing, and it was obvious to people.

Why did the program end after two seasons?
The producer wanted us to continue but also asked us to make changes. The program had started as a Sámi comedy show made for Sámi youth. The channel now wanted us to cater more to a young and hip Finnish audience. This was nothing Kirste and I wanted to do. We didn't want Sámi culture to be some exotic spice for public entertainment. We had already made some compromises for the second season and didn't want to go any further. Kirste and I have talks about doing something together again in the future. We will see. But it would be a different kind of program.

To be a documentary filmmaker and a comedian is not the most common of combinations. Has this confused people?
I think so. I would probably be richer had I branded myself as one or the other, but I hate branding. At some point, I felt I had to choose, but those days are over. I'm happy with where I'm at and with what I do. I feel there's a good balance.

The annual Sámi and indigenous film festival Skábmagovat has been running for more than twenty years in Aanaar, on the Finnish side of Sápmi. How important is the festival for Sámi filmmakers?
Very important. My first films were screened there, and it's still where the films of young Sámi directors get discovered. It also

has a strong international outlook. Every year, there's a focus on a particular indigenous people.

Let us return to your work.
Good. Can I talk about how I work now?

Whatever seems most urgent.
At the moment, I'm really interested in whether it's possible to decolonize filmmaking. Film is such a modern, Western tool, and I'm wondering how to really do a Sámi film, or what that would mean. What would be the method, the approach, and how would the question of ownership be resolved? I've been thinking about this for many years, and I have my ups and downs. Right now, it feels like I've hit rock bottom.

Why?
It just feels impossible. Film is an artistic tool and you need someone with a vision, which usually means a director, but this is far from the Sámi approach to doing things. In our culture, you can't just go ahead and do whatever you feel like; you need permission. So I'm not sure that I can ever use my artistic control as a director in the name of decolonization. At the same time, I find it impossible to continue working according to Western rules and values, so the only option for me is to respect the traditional Sámi ways of thinking and working.

How do you get permission?
I ask permission from the community, from the traditional owners of the story, from the spirits—it feels good, but it is also very exhausting. I sometimes envy my Finnish colleagues, who have no problem going to indigenous communities to collect stories and edit them into a film. I can't do that. Yet I'm always driven by ideas for new projects, so I'm torn between asking permission and going ahead with my plans.

You said you weren't sure what it really means to make a Sámi film. I understand it has to do with how you'd be making the film, but most people would consider *Sami Blood* a Sámi film. Are they wrong?

According to any standard definition of an indigenous film, *Sami Blood* is without a doubt a Sámi film. The writer and director, Amanda Kernell, is Sámi, the main actors are Sámi, it is a film about Sámi culture, and Amanda used stories from her own background. It is a healing tool and one of the most Sámi films ever made. I don't think Amanda has to struggle with whether she did the right thing or not.

About asking permission: I know you mean it in a very broad sense, but you also mentioned asking permission from the community. Won't there always be different opinions?

Yes, but you can't apply Western notions of democracy to Sámi culture. We try to talk until we agree. Consensus is very important. If I ask ten people about a project and one disapproves, I still have great difficulties going through with it. Sometimes, however, I can feel so strongly about a project that I'll do it even if I don't feel that I have full approval—as long as I have received a sign to do it. *Me and My Little Sister* would be an example.

The community didn't want you to make it?

That was the sense I got. People were concerned that Sámi society would be portrayed as homophobic. But I had an inner gut and the approval of queer Sámi. And in this case, their voices were most important to me. It's complicated. I probably shouldn't do this kind of work at all. I really don't like the attention. It's weird that I do it nonetheless.

There's got to be some strong motivating factor.

The urgent need to tell stories and bring issues to the table. Storytelling is my dearest friend. Stories come up in my mind all the time, and I need to get them out, otherwise they eat me up. It's the way I communicate with the world. I find that much easier than entering long debates or whatever else you can do.

What's the story you are working on now?

I'm working on a film about colonialism in Sápmi, particularly on the Finnish side. There has been so much pressure on the Sámi in recent years, it's the only way for me to deal with it. That was also a reason for doing *Me and My Little Sister*. I started the project in the midst of a terrible homophobic wave that swept through Finland and Sápmi. It was my way to contribute to the discussion. I understand that film is a terribly slow tool for that, but I can't deal with discussing this on social media—there's just too much crap. It's easier to collect all the crap and make a film. It's one of the things I love about filmmaking: it gives you time to think and really understand a subject deeply, even if you then present it in a lighter way. It's just so much more than a few comments on Facebook.

How did you get into filmmaking to begin with?
There was a media school that opened in Aanaar, kind of a pilot program, and I instantly fell in love with making documentaries. I had never thought of that before, I didn't even know that documentary filmmaking was a profession. I had no idea that it could be so much more than piecing together war footage, that it allowed you to tell personal stories.

Can you tell us about your involvement in Siidaskuvla?
I feel that we as Sámi people need to have safe spaces to be healed from colonialism and to be empowered. For me, the key answer to this is decolonization. For Sámi, decolonization includes taking back parts of the traditional *siida* system.

On a personal level, it is important for me to learn to think as Sámi as possible. I have already received tremendously valuable information as well as traditional knowledge and values from my Siidaskuvla colleagues. After many years of working mainly with non-Sámi, it has been a heartwarming experience to spend more time with my fellow Sámi. This is a collective I feel at home in.

What parts of the traditional siida system can be helpful for decolonization?
There are many. Which ones work best depends on the person. They can relate to anything from eating habits to spiritual action, from political organizing to a common use of the land. In my own work, the most relevant question is a deep understanding of asking permission and of cooperating with everything that surrounds us, whatever it is. The siida system can also teach us how to handle difficulties among ourselves. I strongly believe in its powers to help our society heal.

Back to your current film project on colonialism. What are you able to reveal?
When will the book come out?

If everything goes as planned, in the spring of 2020.
If everything goes as planned, which it never does, we should be editing the film by then. We still need to secure some more funding, but I'm optimistic. I will focus on the Finnish side of Sápmi because I live here and feel that I can best tell this story to others who live here. The questions raised will be as relevant for Norway, Sweden, and Russia, of course. I don't want to rely on traditional storytelling, with one person at the center. It's the story of a whole nation, and I want to bring in as many people as possible. There is a lot of pain that wants to come out.

Personally or collectively?
Both. I don't think you can separate the two. Since I've had children, I've felt this huge collective pain inside myself, and it needs an outlet. I also have a strong sense that I need to focus on what's best for the world, not just for me.

What is best for the world?
What's best for my kids and all children around the world. I feel I need to work on subjects that really matter.

Is that a burden?
I think that's a Western way of looking at it. I feel that I, as a filmmaker, should do something that helps my people. Some might see this as a burden; I see it as a richness. We Sámi are a collective people. We always think about what's good for all of us, even for the ones we don't like. It is a richness to be part of this people, to be able to serve and share. I'm happy, even if I cry most of the time while working.

The Western world has told us for a long time that individuality is the thing, that you have the right to do whatever you want, to choose your identity, to follow your own path to happiness. But how can I be happy in Helsinki working on comedy panels while reading all the hate speech directed at my people? If someone talks bad about my nation, they talk bad about me, my kids, my father, my sisters. I can't be happy then, no matter how great things are going for me personally. I feel much happier if I am at least trying to do something. And I think it's pretty easy to know when your ego is the motivating factor, or when it's the connection you feel to your people.

I have Finnish colleagues who've tried to relieve me from what they see as a burden. They tell me that it's okay to look out for myself, that I have no obligations. But no Sámi or any other indigenous person has ever told me that. We all feel the same. It's not a burden, it's love.

On your Instagram page it says that you're a "ČSV forever." What does that mean to you?

Most Sámi are ČSV forever. For me, it means that you always do what benefits your people. When you help your people, you help all people.

Karolina

Nils-Olof Parfa

Taken from *Hjärnstorm*, no. 128 (*Samisk vrede*), 2017, 22–24.
Translated from Swedish by G.K.

I longed to find a Sámi girl early on in life. For better or worse. It felt
natural and simple. At the time, I knew very little about life, or love. So
little that it is hard to imagine today. To realize that is perhaps a sign of
age—the first step toward you being the one to tell your story, just as
the elders always have done.

Like so many other Sámi, I grew up with stories about how family
members and relatives found love at the Winter Market in Jåhkåmåhke, a
midsummer dance in Åanghkerenjeeruve, or a Sámi-SM in some obscure
town in Sápmi's hinterland. Every time such an event approached, your
body would let you know. The sensations were very special. So was the
mood of your friends. Everything seemed loaded with static electricity.
The closest comparison I can find is that to a New Year's celebration,
but without the usual disappointment that it wasn't as good as one had
hoped for. As soon as any big Sámi event was over, you were looking
forward to the next one. Many times I left thinking, "Okay, maybe I will
find my big love next time!" After all, finding the right Sámi girl is harder
than you probably think. Perhaps I should explain . . .

There is much to consider when it comes to Sámi dating. The faster
you learn the better! There are many pitfalls and strict rules of behavior.
Family relations are something we Sámi are very careful with. You must
always stay on top of them! Within our community, we are defined by
our last name, our parents, and our wider family. This serves as a social
compass. It's the kind of information you are expected to recite by heart
at any time. The more generations back the better.

A Sámi confirmation is practically obligatory. I don't mean that
our parents force us to do it. It's just that no teenager full of hormones
will want to miss it. It was at a confirmation camp in Vallbo, in the late

1990s, when I had my first longer contact with Sámi youth from outside of Jåhkåmåhke. There and then, I understood the significance of knowing your family. It was both intimidating and exciting. Girls who did not have the same last name as I could still have some of the same relatives. Girls I had cast an eye on turned into a minefield I hardly dared to approach. By the time the camp was over, I was perhaps even more confused than the thrilled thirteen-year-old who had climbed on the bus from Jåhkåmåhke to Jämtland County three weeks earlier. I realized that flirting and a bit of luck wasn't enough. You had to keep track of things and have a lot of luck.

When I was twenty-two, I met the dark-haired South Sámi beauty who I knew had to become mine. It was at a Sámi-SM. In Váhtjer out of all places. Her name was Karolina, a storm from the county of Västerbotten. She had strong opinions and didn't take any crap but appeared frail and vulnerable at the same time. I don't know what she saw in me, but I fell for her directly. This was the beginning of the most beautiful, and most chaotic, time of my life.

Even though we lived almost six hundred kilometers apart, we soon became a couple and presented one another proudly, and nervously, to our friends and families. And we showed one another our mountains and reindeer, of course. I understand that this might sound weird, but it was about us wanting to show each other everything and make each other feel at home and welcome. Besides, everyone around us should know that we were serious. The same applied to the big Sámi events: what had once been an opportunity to find a partner had now become an opportunity for something bigger, namely to present ourselves together.

We soon shared a home and started to plan for a common future—sometimes earnestly, sometimes half-jokingly, and always cautiously. Everything seemed to develop naturally, just like the stories I had grown up with.

Karolina not only showed me new parts of Sápmi, she also revealed another side of Sweden to me. Most of it was wonderful—stories about old friends and places—but some of it was heartbreaking and distressing—stories about racism and the dismal state of mental health services. As Sámi, we had both grown up with insults, threats, and fistfights. That was everyday life, and it hadn't been any different for our parents, grandparents, and many generations before them. But Karolina seemed affected in a way unknown to me. The experiences seemed to eat her up from the inside. I loved her for her frailty. But on some days, she wanted to do nothing but sleep. The effect this had on me was panic. I was upset because I couldn't help her; it was a combination of frustration and anger without any particular direction. It felt terrible to listen to her talk about the hopelessness she felt while trying to comfort her.

I liked being her rock. As I understood much later, there is satisfaction in feeling needed. I liked that my simple presence seemed to help her more than any professional psychiatrist had ever been able to. Yet the circumstances also wore me down.

It took a year before things appeared to take a drastic turn for Karolina. Her new psychiatrist—who even I deemed sensible—felt that it wasn't necessary to continue with their meetings. We were making plans! Karolina wanted to meet her siblings, parents, and other relatives. She was also adamant about returning to where my family kept our reindeer during the summer. She wanted to see the place, Stáloluokta, in the spring. I even got her to eat fish, which I had tried to do since we met. This may appear odd. But—apart from reindeer, of course—I was raised on fish. For my mother's parents, fishing was almost religious. Ice fishing in the spring, net fishing in the summer. Whether the fish was cooked, smoked, or fried didn't matter. I had gotten fish through my mother's milk, and I wanted to share eating fish with Karolina. So I was very happy when she finally agreed. I began to relax.

Then came what I will never forget from that spring. It began on the evening before we had planned to visit Karolina's oldest sister and her family. This was the last point on the wish list she had made after being declared healthy by her psychiatrist. It was only a few days before her twenty-third birthday, and roughly one month before that summer's marking of the calves. Karolina told me a story I hadn't heard before. It scared me more than any of the others. Karolina talked about how she had planned a slow goodbye to her family and all the places she loved. She began to cry. I was terrified. We ended up having a big fight, and I went to bed by myself, angry. I was shocked and hurt. The last thing I said to Karolina before I fell asleep was: "If you leave the house now, you better never come back!" In hindsight, it was an insane way to end an argument and get in the last word. It was both a threat and a childish challenge. But this was nothing I thought of then, in the heat of the moment.

We had been a couple for almost three years. Today, it sounds like a footnote in one's life, but at the time it seemed hard to imagine being thirty years old one day. Three years were like a small eternity. We had had worse fights and said crueler things to one another.

When I woke the next morning, I could feel Karolina's arm around my shoulder. She had not left the house. I was relieved and felt embarrassed. But when I turned around, I realized that Karolina would never come back. She had overdosed on sleeping pills.

For many, to commit suicide is a completely incomprehensible act. Far too often, it is described as an act of cowardice or selfishness. I cannot agree. No matter how deeply I mourned Karolina, I was never angry at her. I believe that people who feel so low don't see anything but darkness and imagine themselves to be a burden for everyone. To take your own life means having conviction.

Shock has an incredibly strong impact on your body and your mind. It is impossible to know in advance how you'll react. I became mechanical. I switched between giving CPR and making emergency calls and was in total denial. I simply could not accept that Karolina was dead. It seemed impossible that I had woken up beside her for the last time.

When an ambulance finally reached us, it felt like the whole world came crushing down. Had I gotten any kind of warning, or had I just kept my composure that evening, it might still be the two of us today. I would have certainly said something different, perhaps made a clumsy attempt at being poetic or offering something deep. I would have avoided a fight. But the truth is, I'm afraid that no one can plan for anything like this. Not in reality.

Only after Karolina had died, did I really understand the hopelessness she had talked about so often. I lost my appetite and didn't want to leave the bed. And I experienced for myself a mental health system that lacks any understanding or empathy, an institution that had let Karolina down.

The short crisis management I got was almost comical. During the second of three scheduled meetings, I was threatened with having my sick leave withdrawn when I mentioned wanting to join my family in Stáloluokta for the marking of the calves. It felt like being kicked when you're already down. "Calf marking in the summer? Everyone knows that Sámi mark their calves in the fall! Besides, you've gotta understand that I can't let you work when you're on sick leave." With such words echoing in my head, it was an easy decision to let my family take care of me instead. The friends I grew up with gave me the support the professionals were obviously unable to give. Meanwhile, my relatives reminded me of old stories and heartbreak, of newfound love, and of well-deserved happiness.

I realized I had two options: one was to give in and get buried in sorrow; the other was to embrace love and continue to live. I chose the latter. And I chose my memories of Karolina. For better or worse. They are with me while searching for the next big love.

Anders Sunna

Photo courtesy of Anders Sunna

Anders Sunna (1985) has spearheaded a new wave of political Sámi art. He has had numerous exhibitions in Sápmi and the Nordic countries and is widely regarded as one of the most innovative contemporary artists of the region. You can find much of his work at www.anderssunna.com and follow him on Instagram: @anders_sunna. I visited him in his studio in Jåhkåmåhke in May 2019.

Why is art so closely tied to politics in Sámi culture?
Art is a part of daily life in a Sámi family. All children draw, everyone tells stories, and you're being creative with whatever is at hand. There are many advantages with using art to express yourself. You don't need to share a language with someone, and your message travels fast and far. No political party can do the same. And you don't need to stick to any party platform either. For me, art is the perfect tool to communicate, to make people aware, and to change things.

You're often mentioned as a prime example for a new generation of Sámi artists. But how "new" is this generation compared to the Sámi artists who came before?
All artists have their own characteristics. But I feel that, for a long time, Sámi artists had a tendency to follow the same patterns. They always looked at what other Sámi artists did. It almost seemed as if people were scared of doing something different. There is nothing wrong with that per se, but I wanted something more. I was looking for inspiration beyond Sámi art while making sure I stayed true to my historical background. If you don't dare to look outside—always with Sámi eyes, of course—there is no development. Sámi culture is no exhibit in a museum. We are a living people, and our culture needs to be alive, develop, and change.

One feature of this so-called new generation is the militant imagery used: weapons, balaclavas, barricades . . .
Yes, these are elements that I introduced.

Why?
My family has been castigated as terrorists for a long time. That's reflected in my art. But it's also important to look at the details. I don't just use any weapons. When I use a Kalashnikov, the symbolism is very clear: it's a weapon of rebellion—and it shows what can happen if you oppress people for too long.

The history of Sámi resistance has not been militant. Are you sending a warning?
You can see it that way. If you take a group of people and oppress them and take away their rights, there will be an explosion at some

point. Or let's say, there are only two options: implosion or explosion. All I'm saying is: how long do you think you can oppress these people without there being consequences?

The usual story is that much progress has been made in the past thirty years.

But that story is not true. Yes, everyone refers to the Sámi parliaments and whatnot, but the truth is, nothing has changed. The Sámi parliaments have no power. In Sweden, the Sámi Parliament is subordinate to the Ministry for Rural Affairs. Essentially, it has nothing to say. It was set up by the Swedish state and is modeled after colonial political institutions. Being dependent on the Swedish state, Sámi politicians always have to be worried about losing funding. And whenever Sámi politicians do get to decide something, they look out for their own interests first. This also means that they help the state to get rid of "Sámi troublemakers"—people like my family.

The crucial question is: How do we, as Sámi, treat one another? There is a lot of talk about solidarity, but I see very little of it. We can talk about decolonization all we want, but it's not going to help us if we don't find an answer to that question. Decolonization happens from the inside out and from the bottom to the top. Everything has to come from your heart.

You have said that your political struggle is a marathon, not a sprint. What do you mean?

You need to be in it for the long run. There is no overnight solution. It's more like water dripping on a stone. Eventually, there'll be a hole, but it's going to take a long time. Many Sámi activists get burned out, because they have no long-term strategy. We easily fall victim to colonial thinking and believe that everything has to happen at the drop of a hat. But we're up against a power that has many resources: people, money, and time. You can't buy time and you'll never get any back. It is important to know your enemy.

How has the marathon been going so far?

There are some effects. When I started out, people thought I was crazy. Now, people say they are inspired by my work and copy me. It's going all right.

A marathon is long. Is there a particular goal?
There is always a goal, but you have to get there, and that's the hard part.

But what is the goal? What will life be like for the Sámi when they are no longer oppressed?
We will be involved in making the decisions that affect our lives. We will have the right to stop the destruction of our natural resources and to live our lives the way we want to. But we will also stop judging one another by whether we own reindeer or speak Sámi. We will be one people, standing up for one another, not being divided by envy.

Do the national borders make for special obstacles?
I actually don't think so. When we realize that we are one people and act as such, these borders are not going to stop us. But unity is mandatory. You can't hop over necessary steps toward self-determination just to get there faster. There are no shortcuts. If you try to find one, there is always a price to pay. We need to take one step at a time, be thoughtful, and advance on our terms, not those of the state.

Do you use the term "artivism"?
No, I don't use any such words. They don't mean anything to me. I am the person I am, and I do what I do. I hardly even refer to myself as an "artist." People create categories out of insecurity. They feel the need to belong, and they like to think they know someone even if they don't. Categorization reflects a colonial mind-set. People aren't allowed to be who they are. Besides, the whole activist thing has become watered down so much that the word, or any variation of it, hardly means anything these days. Everyone wants to be an activist.

Do you have a particular audience in mind when you work on your art?
No, I never think of an audience. Once you start thinking about others or about commercial aspects, you stop being true to yourself. You need a solid basis to stand on. That's also the only way to stand for what you do. My most important critic is my heart, as it is my heart that I can't betray.

You mentioned your family's conflict with the Swedish state. I understand it's a complex issue, but can it be summarized?

When people think of reindeer herding in Sweden, they think of Sámi. But you can actually own up to thirty reindeer even if you're not Sámi. This goes back to a law from the eighteenth century that was supposed to attract settlers to the north. Today, people make use of it because they think it's fun to own reindeer or because they get a tax deduction. But while these people may own reindeer, Sámi reindeer herders are still supposed to take care of them. Special samebyar exist for this kind of arrangement, so-called concession samebyar.

And the Sámi reindeer herders get paid for that work?

No, that's the point. Sometimes, they even have to pay the Swedish hobby reindeer owners to use their land. It's a messed-up arrangement, and my family refused to partake in it. In 1971, the board members of the sameby we belonged to, which is a concession sameby, informed the Swedish authorities. They felt that we were creating too much trouble. This is when the conflict escalated. Its beginnings lie in the 1930s, when we were called "crazy communists."

Why?

I guess you called everyone you didn't agree with a "crazy communist" at the time. My family was never very political.

And the conflict remains unresolved?

It remains unresolved. We were expelled from the sameby and forced to take care of our reindeer outside the law.

Is your case special?

It's special because all of this has been going on for close to fifty years, and we have had to deal with so much repression. Not only were the police after us all the time, but so were other people. Some of the teachers of my siblings and me owned reindeer and made sure we got bad grades. When we went grocery shopping in town, there was always the possibility that someone would slash our tires. We never felt safe. People usually have a hard time believing that anything like this could happen in Sweden, but it has been our reality for a long time. And we haven't gotten much help at all, neither from Sámi nor from non-Sámi. And when there was help, it was ignored: there were 130 Swedish property owners in our area who signed a statement declaring that they wanted our family's Sámi reindeer herding and not some hobby reindeer herding, but the authorities didn't react, and this wasn't reported by the media either.

But according to your explanation, there must be other families in the same situation: taking care of others' reindeer without being compensated for it. What's the difference between them and your family?
We spoke up. We refused to do what we were told to do. Others preferred to be the "good Sámi" and obey the state. We became a problem even for them.

You said there wasn't any help from non-Sámi either. It's always been surprising to me how little interest there is in Sápmi among Swedish activists. Many other causes seem more important. Why?
First of all, they don't know anything about Sápmi. The schools don't teach anything. Second, Swedish people are very insecure. If no one else raises their hand, they won't either. Finally, Sámi issues are complicated, and it seems easiest not to get involved.

People on the Swedish side of Sápmi often describe a rather harsh climate between Sámi and non-Sámi, more so than in the neighboring countries. For an outsider it's maybe not so obvious, but how would you describe it?
You know what people think, and you might watch what you say depending on who's around—or you don't, if you don't care. But it differs from place to place, too. I now live in Jåhkåmåhke, and it's a breeze compared to Bájil, where I grew up. Then again, if you compare Jåhkåmåhke to Stockholm, Jåhkåmåhke might seem terrible. It's all relative.

When it comes to controversial issues—anything from snowmobile driving to economic policies—it doesn't seem that you have two clear-cut camps, Sámi and non-Sámi. Opinions often seem to be across the board.

The Sámi are divided on many issues. The Swedish state has caused many of these divisions through the legal distinction between reindeer herders and other Sámi. This has basically created a Sámi class society: some Sámi are better than others. Furthermore, you have people who aren't Sámi but who "feel" Sámi. But what does that feel like?

You were talking about right steps at the right time. What's the next one?

Respect one another, help one another, create unity.

About the Painting "Area Infected"

Anders Sunna

Taken from www.anderssunna.com. (See the full-color insert for the painting.) Translated from Swedish by G.K.

It was in the summer of 1986. I was just one year old when it happened. I had not been part of the conflict from when it all began, in 1972, but the events impacted my entire life. If you grow up with a conflict all around you, it follows you wherever you go. The abnormal becomes your normal.

My father has told us everything he could about that summer in Paskarova, a place outside the village of Anttis, not far from Bájil. What unfolded that summer is portrayed in the painting. But the work does not simply refer to the past. It offers an image of the present, of how children are affected by the decisions of adults and politicians. It raises the question of how future generations can be completely disregarded.

The background to the events is the reindeer-herding law of 1971 and its misinterpretation. The law contributed to the impression that Sámi concession owners had an obligation to take care of reindeer owned by non-Sámi landowners. In exchange, the Sámi were allowed to use the landowners' property for herding. Eventually, this interpretation of the law was declared illegal, but it was made legal again by a 2006 amendment to the law. Our family opposed this because we didn't consider it reasonable to take care of others' reindeer without compensation. For us, it amounted to slave labor. As a consequence, the entire family was persecuted. This caused a conflict that split our sameby into two camps. In 1978, the authorities in Norrbotten County canceled all reindeer marks registered by families who were on our side. In 1981, we were told to move our reindeer from the sameby of Sattajärvi to that of Mounio. The move was supposed to be monitored by a police patrol and the reindeer owners from Sattajärvi who wanted to get rid of us.

In the summer of 1986, the police and a group of reindeer owners came to our pastures during the marking of the calves. They told us that it was their duty to move all reindeer to Mounio, if necessary by force. These particular reindeer owners had already in 1983 tried to persuade the Norrbotten authorities to ordain the forced culling of our reindeer. Now, they could hide their true intentions, as they could claim that they were simply leading our reindeer to Mounio. Taxpayers' money had been used to build a thirty-kilometer fence to prevent our reindeer from returning to our lands. My father, his brothers, and the reindeer owners supporting us resisted. But once the reindeer became thirsty, they had to be moved. During the journey, hundreds of them disappeared. There was a slaughterhouse no farther than ten kilometers away. Many years later, one of the people involved admitted that many of our reindeer were taken there.

Since the authorities didn't want to be accused of forced displacement, they claimed that we had sought permission to join Mounio. This is untrue. They probably wanted to distract from their actions and create strife among our people. We've been forced to engage in guerrilla herding ever since. We can't be heard or seen. We have no permanent facilities. We build fences just before we need them—for example for the marking of the calves—and take them down as soon as we are done. We operate entirely outside the system. This means, among other things, no compensation for reindeer killed by predators.

When you grow up feeling constantly persecuted and when you experience how Swedish politics work, it is easy to lose your belief in Swedish society. It becomes impossible to identify with it. But we have also lost our trust in the Sámi community, since no one stood up for us, neither the National Association of Sámi in Sweden nor the Sámi Parliament. They take an embarrassing bow to colonialism's suit-wearing politicians and their insatiable appetite for natural resources and power.

I remember how worried my mother was when our father and his brothers were in the reindeer forest. She used to pace up and down, and the longer it took for them to come home the more anxious she became, wondering whether they would return at all or be found shot dead. During the worst periods, it was indeed that bad.

I am grateful to my parents that they always told us everything. We children were part of the struggle from our birth. We weren't kept in the dark but rather seen as a resource. I understood this in my teenage years, when art became the weapon I told our story with, trying to create change. If someone hands you a text, you can choose to read it or not. It can only touch you emotionally if you understand it and have the time that requires. An image, on the other hand, causes a direct reaction and stirs up emotions quickly, positive or negative. Images leave an impression etched on your memory.

I still hope that our family will get the justice we deserve. But I understand that when you are up against the state, there is a difference between *being* right and being *treated* right. Our trust in the Swedish justice system is nonexistent. People say that we live in a democracy in Sweden, but I have experienced something different. I am a stateless person in a dictatorship. Not only was the right to reindeer herding taken away from us, but it was also handed to others who have no historical connection to it. Our family has herded reindeer longer than anyone can remember. We might have been able to accept a complete change of policy, but how our rights can simply be given to someone else is hard to comprehend.

I understand the pain that Sámi feel who have lost their right to reindeer herding generations ago. To have that right taken away from you brutally, and to grow up with that experience, is like having your heart ripped out and put on display in a glass bowl. What this causes inside of you is something to reckon with: you need an outlet for your anger and frustration; the lust for revenge makes your blood pump like an adrenaline shot; you seek ways to control yourself, not to become too militant, not to go berserk. Art has been my savior.

After all those years, after everything we had to go through and are still going through, my parents were asked by a journalist how we've been able to cope with it. My mother said: "You survive, but you don't live."

Maxida Märak

Photo: Patrik Lindén

Maxida Märak (born 1988) is a recording artist, producer, actress, and political activist who is one of the most prominent voices from Sápmi in Sweden today. She has collaborated with indigenous artists such as Bill Miller and A Tribe Called Red and was a key figure in the protests against mining in Gállok, near her hometown of Jåhkåmåhke. In the fall of 2019, her solo album *Utopi* was released. You can follow Maxida on Instagram: @maxidamarak. We met in Stockholm in July 2019.

Can you tell us about Tjáhppis rájddo?
It was a group protesting the mining plans in Gállok. A friend and I talked about how we had to do something during the 2014 Jåhkåmåhke Winter Market. The winter market is a big event, with thousands of tourists arriving and much media attention. We were disgusted by how the Jåhkåmåhke authorities used Sámi culture to advertise the event, when they had just approved test drilling in Gállok and disregarded all of the reindeer herders' concerns. It felt like they were spitting in our faces.

As we talked, we realized we had to do something that hadn't been done before, something powerful. Demonstrations are great, but it's easy for people to simply look the other way. It's rare that they alone make a big difference. The same goes for petitions. The officials in Jåhkåmåhke were fully aware of the consequences of their decision; they just didn't care.

So we looked at the single biggest feature of the market, the one that gets the most attention, and that's the reindeer caravan. It is great, but the truth is, there won't be any more reindeer caravans for real in the Jåhkåmåhke area if there will indeed be a mine. You can see that in other parts of Sápmi where mining has taken over. So we decided to do a "black reindeer caravan," which is what *tjáhppis rájddo* means in Lule Sámi. We found people willing to join us, we tamed some reindeer, we sewed Sámi dresses out of black garbage bags, and when the day of the market came, we were ready.

How was the action received?
It got a lot of attention. It was very successful. We made people across Sweden aware of how the state was treating the Sámi, and we encouraged others—Sámi and non-Sámi—to speak up. But it was also very intense. We could feel the hatred of many folks as soon as we stepped into the market.

What happened to the group afterward?
It split up pretty soon. You have to understand the consequences of doing something like this in a small community. It's easy for big-city folks to point fingers at people who take a step back or want to be anonymous, but they don't understand the repercussions. In a place like Jåhkåmåhke, everyone knows everyone, and you are dependent on many people. The person who saw you at

the protest might be your boss or your doctor or the clerk you will meet next time you go to the social office. In other words, being part of an action like this can affect your entire life. If you have money and powerful contacts, you can probably deal with it, but as a single mom with three kids and one job to rely on, you're taking enormous risks. Me, I was spat at and basically ostracized. You can always try to brush things off and say you don't give a shit, but we all have a heart and a soul. These are people I went to school with. It gets to you.

So, Tjáhppis rájddo no longer exists?
The core people still stick together and can mobilize for further actions. But the group itself is not really what's important. What's important is that we inspired people across Sápmi, especially young people, who are now doing similar things. They saw that you can have an impact. We've been raised believing that there is no point in speaking up, that it's only going to make things worse. But if you are persistent, you can change things, even as an individual.

In 2014–2015, you did a tour with your sibling Timimie, performing in town halls and gymnasiums of small communities across Sápmi. Is this anything you'd consider doing today, when you can fill concert halls anywhere in Sweden?
Yes, not least because it's a matter of justice. My songs have a message, and I need to live up to it. I find it disheartening that so many artists on my level don't care about that audience. I know that some of the kids who saw us on that tour still listen to my music. They are politically conscious and active. It makes me very proud. I had been one of them! I know how hard it is to go to shows when you live in small, isolated communities, so when an artist makes the effort to go there and inspire just one person, it's epic! There are issues that complicate things, like that I'm living off my music today and can't do too many things for no pay, but I still do shows like that when I can. If there is any place you need to take your message, it's there.

You have spoken of a "war in Norrbotten," the northernmost county of Sweden where most of the Sámi live. Is the social climate really that tense?
Yes, I think so.

Anders Sunna says that it's different from place to place. For example, it's worse in Giron and Bájil than in Jåhkåmåhke.

I would agree with that, and it also shows the impact that mining and big industry have. There's a very raw climate in a place like Giron. I lived there for a couple of years, working at the Sámi theater. In Jåhkåmåhke, there are three strong samebyar, the water is clean, and the mountains remain untouched. Despite everything I've experienced, I love Jåhkåmåhke. But even there, the community is divided. It's rare to see Swedish kids hang out with Sámi kids. People stick to their own circles. But it's not as rough as the mining towns are.

There is a slogan that's popular among some Swedish activists, "Autonomt Norrland," expressing sympathy with Sweden's northern counties, which are neglected by the central government. However, even if these counties had autonomy, would it help the Sámi? Local governments have been as repressive historically, sometimes more. Does the slogan speak to you?

I don't use it, and I don't know much about the people who do, so I'm not going to pass judgment on them either. But I can say something about activist groups in general. You have to be careful with people who love to stand on the front lines, raise their fists, and yell louder than anyone else. They often forget why they are so-called activists in the first place. Activism—a word I've come to feel very uncomfortable with—is not about being cool or having a bit of fun. It's about changing things. And getting into fights is not always the best thing to do.

The starting point for getting people on our side is to be kind and respectful. And you have to leave your bubble. I decided to go to the places of power and stand eye to eye with the politicians who govern our lives. And I decided to treat them with respect—not the far-right Sweden Democrats, but everyone else—in order to earn their respect. I have become friends with many of them. The next time they'll have to address a question that concerns my people, they'll be thinking of me. And there is a good chance that this will influence their decision—much more so than had I just spat at them. Why would that make them decide in the interest of my people?

Most activists don't want to go there. But if you're serious about politics, you must be smart and choose what's most effective. It's not always the yelling.

I get the impression that you are very generous with people and the mistakes they make. That's not so common in activist circles.
You have to be generous. Let's be honest with ourselves. Do I know everything about Islam? No. But how am I going to learn if I have to be afraid that someone will call me a racist if I ask a dumb question? Yes, it is unjust and tiresome to have to respond to dumb questions and to have to explain yourself all the time, but you know what? The world is unjust. It would be wonderful if everyone was knowledgeable about everything, but that's not the case. People in Sweden weren't supposed to know anything about my people; it was part of the colonial strategy. I can't be angry at them for that. If someone uses a racial slur, that's different. But if someone asks me how many reindeer I own or whether I live in a tent, they are often just curious. I use the opportunity to educate them. If you give them a hard time for it, it's unlikely they'll learn.

You said you've become friends with many politicians across the political spectrum, but you've also made it clear in interviews that you stand on the left. However, the Left in Sweden hasn't necessarily been more on the Sámi's side than others, has it?
No one is on the Sámi's side. When I say that I belong to the Left, it's in the context of Swedish politics. I believe in solidarity and justice. As far as the interests of the Sámi are concerned, however, the left parties don't necessarily have the best program.

What do you mean?
Look at the Greens: they try to be conscious of Sámi rights, and that's very good. But many of the policies they support affect the Sámi in negative ways—or anyone living in the far north, for that matter. People are dependent on cars, snowmobiles, and helicopters, and running your own business is a lifeline for many. No single political party has the solutions.

The media has turned you into a spokesperson for your people, whether you like that role or not. Do you ever feel that this has a negative impact on the artist Maxida Märak?
In the beginning it was very annoying. Not only was I always the "Sámi artist" but the "Sámi woman artist." Fuck you! I'm an artist and a producer. My ethnicity and my gender are not my first

names. Don't get me wrong: I'm proud that I get to speak about my people and that I have an audience. But there is a time for everything. Sometimes it's important that I'm a Sámi, and sometimes not at all.

Have things improved?
With the media? Absolutely. But it was a struggle. I had to discuss the issue with journalists many times.

You have also spoken about the responsibility that comes with having an audience. Does that put much pressure on you? Like, do you feel you have to say something important in every interview, while sometimes it might just be nice to babble?
I get to babble when I want to. Of course there are times when I can't be bothered talking politics, say, when I'm with my friends or at a party. But in an interview like this one? I'd be an idiot not to use the opportunity to talk about issues that are important to me. No, no pressure. There are other things to worry about.

I've come across people who have raised the question of how "representative" you are for the Sámi community. I guess you don't fit their idea of what a Sámi has to be like and seem "too modern" or something. How do you respond to that?
People have opinions about me all the time, and there is little I can do. Some people don't like that I have a platform and want me to be quiet. Questioning my credibility is an easy way to attack me. Obviously, no single Sámi can speak for all Sámi. I cannot represent an entire people every time I open my mouth. I have never claimed to do that. I voice my personal opinions, which are the opinions of a Sámi, and I'm proud if that helps raise awareness about the injustices that Sámi people face.

In your lifetime, what do you feel has changed for the Sámi community?
I think it's beneficial for us that Sweden has become more multicultural. People in Sweden have begun to understand that it's not bizarre or inferior if you live in a different way, speak a different language, or have a different religion. Today, they realize that the world is diverse and they start to understand how badly the Sámi

have been treated by the Swedish state. There have been improvements in education, and we have gotten access to institutions we were excluded from before. The problem is that we don't have much time left to turn things around for everyone. Our resources are running out, and it's soon game over. Once you have built too many mines and destroyed the land, there is no way back. This really concerns me.

Any chance to still turn things around?
Call me naive, but I believe in the good of people. We always assume that people are bad. Why? We all have hearts, and if you touch a person's heart, you can change that person. I believe that humanity will realize how much there is to learn from indigenous peoples. It becomes so obvious that what we have said for centuries is true: if you don't treat nature with respect, it will come back to haunt you. I have to believe that we can still turn things around. Otherwise, I'd have to give up fighting.

The Saami Manifesto 15

Read out at the 2015 Jåhkåmåhkke Winter Market, February 6. English version taken from www.idlenomore.ca.

We live and work for this . . .

1. Because we have to. Because this is the only way of life we know.

2. Because everything begins and ends with *Eanan*, mother, land. *Eanan* is the base for everything. *Eanan* is the question and the answer. Nothing defines us better than her. Our survival depends on her. It is our responsibility to protect, respect and take care of our mother, so that we, and all the generations to come, can live as one with her. Reconnected.

3. Because we have the inherent right to self-determination and freedom in our land. Without these rights we are suffering. It is the time for our people to start living instead of just surviving. We want to live, not die.

4. Because our mother tongues are the mirrors of our worldviews and an essential part of our identity. By preserving and developing our mother tongues we preserve and develop our identities as well as ourselves. Weakened state of language undermines the ability to communicate. The Sámi languages are endangered today. We therefore demand that all the Sámi are given the needed resources and the respect in order to preserve and develop the Sámi languages. When a language is disappearing, it is a sign of the nature and the animals disappearing with it. We demand protection for our *Eanan*, land, culture and our Indigenous languages in order to be able to develop the same way as all other peoples should be allowed to develop.

5. Because we are disconnected from the mother Earth and therefore we feel powerless. When reconnected, we avoid self-destructiveness through love for life and freedom to act for it. The power is to be able to preserve and develop life. We need to reconnect with *Eanan*, the Earth. People all around the globe should reflect on their relationship with nature. One neither gains the freedom in life until one is given the freedom to live, nor does one gain the freedom in death until one is given the freedom to die.

6. Because non-existent people are not granted any rights. We do not want to be ignored anymore, we want to be respected as an Indigenous people also by the Swedish and Finnish governments in these national areas. Sweden and Finland should ratify the ILO 169 and implement the United Nations Declaration on the Rights of Indigenous Peoples. Respect Indigenous peoples' rights to self-determination and existence. Exploiters and their supporters shall know that the shamefulness of their doings will not be kept in silence.

7. Because we believe there will be no change without protest. We all have the power to act and change things today. This is a call for gathering, mobilization and action, revolution and decolonization. It is time for liberation.

8. Because our connection to the land should be passed on to our offspring. This is essential in order to follow the old path of light. We do this for freedom, justice and a better future. These are human rights.

9. Let our voice be followed by the waves of echoes. Let courage encourage courage.

Anders Sunna, Jenni Laiti, Niillas Holmberg, Max Mackhe, Maxida Märak, Mimie Märak

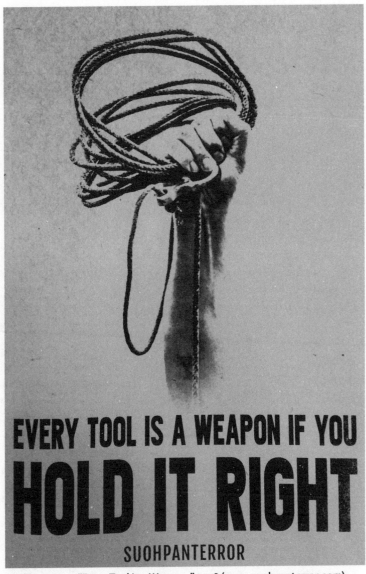

Suohpanterror, "Every Tool Is a Weapon," 2018 (www.suohpanterror.com).

Appendix: English-Language Resources

Literature

Historically inclined readers should be able to find a copy of *The History of Lapland* (1674), the English-language edition of Johannes Schefferus's *Lapponia*, at a university library. Sámi scholars describe it as a remarkably apt account of Sámi culture, most certainly owed to the input of Sámi poet Olaus Sirma, who was the author's most important source.

Much of the modern literature on the Sámi (or "Lapps," as they were called in English for a long time) is dominated by travelogues of European writers. They are all marked by the exotifying gaze characteristic of European travel literature, although to different degrees. Examples reach from Paul B. Du Chaillu's *Land of the Midnight Sun* (2 vols., 1881–1882) and Emilie Demand Hatt's *With the Lapps in the High Mountains: A Woman among the Sami, 1907–1908* (original Danish edition 1913, English edition 2013) to Marie Herbert's *The Reindeer People: Travels in Lapland* (1976) and Hugh Beach's *Guest of the Reindeer Herders* (1993). In its own class is *An Account of the Sámi* by reindeer herder Johan Turi, considered the first-ever secular work published in Sámi (1910, English edition 2011).

After World War II, several ethnological studies were published, mostly authored by non-Sámi writers, among them Ian Whitaker's *Social Relations in a Nomadic Lappish Community* (1955), Roberto Bosi's *The Lapps* (1960), Tom G. Svensson's *Ethnicity and Mobilization in Sami Politics* (1976), and Tom Ingold's *The Skolt Lapps Today* (1976). Important contributions came from the Sámi scholars Israel Ruong, *The Lapps in Sweden* (1967), and Karl Nickul, *The*

Lappish Nation: Citizens of Four Countries (1977). Rowland G.P. Hill's *The Lapps To-day in Finland, Norway and Sweden* (1960) documents the first Sámi Conferences.

Due to the Áltá crisis, books about the Sámi published in the 1980s and '90s often had a political focus. Examples include Piers Vitebsky's *Threatened Cultures: Saami of Lapland* (1993), Trond Thuen's *Quest for Equity: Norway and the Saami Challenge* (1995), and Dave Lewis's awkwardly titled *Indigenous Rights Claims in Welfare Capitalist Society: Recognition and Implementation: The Case of the Sami People in Norway, Sweden and Finland* (1996).

Books in English by Sámi authors also became more readily available. Nils-Aslak Valkeapää's *Greetings from Lappland: The Sami—Europe's Forgotten People* appeared in English in 1983 (original Finnish edition 1971). Three collections of Valkeapää's poetry have also been published in English, *Trekways of the Wind* (1994), *The Sun, My Father* (1997), and *The Earth, My Mother* (2017). *The Sun, My Father* is the English edition of *Beaivi, áhčážan*, for which Valkeapää received the Nordic Council's Literature Prize in 1991.

One of Valkeapää's translators, literary historian Harald Gaski, edited the groundbreaking anthology *Sami Culture in a New Era: The Norwegian Sami Experience* (1997). Gaski is also the editor of *In the Shadow of the Midnight Sun: Contemporary Sami Prose and Poetry* (1996), *Time Is a Ship That Never Casts Anchor: Sami Proverbs* (2006), and *Myths, Tales and Poetry from Four Centuries of Sámi Literature* (2019).

Introductions into Sámi culture were provided by Odd Mathis Hætta, *The Sami: An Indigenous People of the Arctic* (1993); Sunna Kuoljok and John E. Utsi, *The Saami: People of the Sun and Wind* (1993); Veli-Pekka Lehtola, *The Sámi People: Traditions in Transition* (2002); and Ulla-Maija Kulonen, Irja Seurujärvi-Kari, and Risto Pulkkinen, *The Saami: A Cultural Encyclopaedia* (2005).

In 2008, Vuokko Hirvonen's *Voices from Sápmi: Sámi Women's Path to Authorship*, the first doctoral thesis written in Sámi (1998), was published in English. *In Between Worlds* (2016) is the English edition of a Máret Ánne Sara tale that was nominated for the 2014 Nordic Council Children and Young People's Literature Prize. In 2015, Ellen Marie Jensen's *What We Believe In: Sámi Religious Experience and Beliefs from 1593 to the Present* was published. *The Way Back* (2016) is a collection of Niillas Holmberg poems in English translation.

The end of the Soviet Union brought renewed research in the Sámi community on the Russian side of Sápmi, resulting in publications such as *Sami Potatoes: Living with Reindeer and Perestroika* (1998) by Michael P. Robinson and Karim-Ali Kassam and *Running with Reindeer: Encounters in Russian Lapland* (2003) by Roger Took. The latest decade has seen some lavish books about Sápmi published in English, including *Queering Sápmi: Indigenous Stories Beyond the Norm* (2014), the text and picture collection *Visions of Sápmi* (2015), and *Sámi Art and Aesthetics: A Contemporary Perspective* (2017). Victoria Harnesk's *Taste of Sápmi—Sámi Cuisine* (2015) is an award-winning cookbook originally published in Swedish.

A photo book of a special kind is *The People under the Northern Lights* (2019), a collection of colorized pictures taken by Danish photographer Sophus Tromholt in 1882–1883. Also captivating is Erika Larsen's *Sàmi: Walking with Reindeer* (2013). No English captions are included in Oyvind Ravna's *Boazodoallosámit/Reindriftssamer* (2007) and Lena Stenberg's *Sápmi 2000* (2014), but the books are well worth consulting for the images alone. *Mari Moments* (2017), edited by Susanne Hætta, is a photographic biography of Mari Boine.

The reader of the 2012 "RE:Mindings conference" organized by May-Britt Öhman can be downloaded under the title *RE:Mindings: Co-constituting Indigenous/Academic/Artistic Knowledges* at the Uppsala University website (https://uu.diva-portal.org/smash/get/diva2:734635/FULLTEXT01.pdf). A digital version of Aslak Holmberg's thesis *Bivdit Luosa—To Ask for Salmon: Saami Traditional Knowledge on Salmon and the River Deatnu: In Research and Decision-making* (2018) is available at the website of the University of Tromsø—Arctic University of Norway (https://munin.uit.no/handle/10037/12868). Holmberg has also summarized the Deatnu River protests and the colonial context they emerged in under the title "Ellos Deatnu!—Long Live the River Deatnu! Indigenous Sámi People's Struggle for Self-Determination" for the book *A Greater Miracle* (2019), edited by the Miracle Workers Collective.

The English catalog version of the exhibition *Let the River Flow: The Sovereign Will and the Making of a New Worldliness* can be accessed digitally at the website of the Office for Contemporary Art Norway (https://www.oca.no/publications/project-booklets/let-the-river-flow-the-sovereign-will-and-the-making-of-a-new-worldliness-english/). The 54-page catalog for the *Sami Reindeer People of Alaska* exhibition can be ordered from the Sami Cultural Center of North America (www.samiculturalcenter.org).

There are two books documenting the Sámi emigration to North America: *Sámi Reindeer Herders in Alaska: Letters from America 1901–1937* (2014), edited by Aage Solbakk and John Trygve Solbakk, and *We Stopped Forgetting: Stories from Sámi Americans* (2014), edited by Ellen Marie Jensen.

Film

Sápmi possesses a world-renowned film director in Nils Gaup, whose film *Pathfinder*, a historical action movie based on a Sámi legend, was nominated for the Academy Award for Best Foreign Language Film in 1987. Gaup's *Kautokeino Rebellion* (2008) is a nuanced and visually stunning depiction of the 1852 Sámi uprising in Guovdageaidnu.

The Sámi film that has received most attention in recent years is *Sami Blood* (2016), directed by Amanda Kernell. Based on the life story of Kernell's grandmother, it is a powerful depiction of the colonization of Sápmi, carried by a spellbinding performance of lead actress Lene Cecilia Sparrok.

The "Nordic noir" TV series *Midnight Sun* (2016) has been hailed as a mainstream media portrayal of Sámi culture beyond common stereotypes, even if that perception is not shared by everyone. The series features Sámi artists such as Sofia Jannok and Maxida Märak but is not a Sámi production.

There is a broad selection of documentary films about Sápmi, some of which have reached audiences beyond the Nordic countries, for example *The Tundra Settlers* (2004), portraying a Danish-German couple of silversmiths in Guovdageaidnu; *Jojk* (2014), exploring the unique Sámi singing tradition; and *Sound of the Sami Plains* (2017), a behind-the-scenes look at the annual Sámi Grand Prix song contest. *The Wind Is Blowing through My Heart* (2013) is a tribute to Nils-Aslak Valkeapää with English subtitles. *Son of the Sun* (2017) is also a portrayal of Valkeapää, based on interviews with people who knew him.

Jon, the Sami (2010) follows the life of a reindeer-herding family in the Sarek Mountains, while *The Last Generation? Sami Reindeer Herders in Swedish Lapland* (2013) documents the work of

Forest Sámi Hendrik Andersson. Tor Tuorda's *På flytt: en naturfilm om renskötsel* (In Motion: A Natural History Film about Reindeer Herding, 2009) lacks English subtitles but includes hardly any dialogue—the images speak for themselves. *All Aboard! The Sleigh Ride* (2015) is a BBC production following Sámi reindeer herders on a two-hour reindeer sleigh ride in real time.

Skolt Sámi director Katja Gauriloff has received much praise for her films *A Shout into the Wind* (2007), the portrayal of a Skolt Sámi family, and *Kaisa's Enchanted Forest* (2016), a documentary about the friendship between her great-grandmother, the story-teller Kaisa Taisia Gauriloff, and the Swiss writer Robert Crottet. *Me and My Little Sister* (2016) is the most widely distributed of Suvi West's many documentary films.

Give Us Our Skeletons (1999) follows Niillas Somby's quest to retrieve the skull of his ancestor Mons Aslaksen Somby, one of the two Sámi executed for their role in the Guovdageaidnu Rebellion. The website minusplato.com offers a comprehensive selection of video material by and about Somby (https://minusplato.com/2018/10/freedom-park-fridays-niillas-life-work.html).

Highly recommended is the *Thinking at the Edge of the World* series (2016–2017). It includes short films with Niillas Somby, Synnøve Persen, Hans Ragnar Mathisen, and Máret Ánne Sara. The films are available on the website of the Office for Contemporary Art Norway (https://oca.no/programme/notations/thinking-at-the-edge-of-the-world.perspectives-from-the-north.1).

English subtitles have been added to an abbreviated version of the documentary film *Alta saken* (The Alta Case, 1982) and to *The Gállok Rebellion* (2013), produced by protesters themselves. At the time of writing, both films were accessible for free online. So was Aslak Holmberg's excellent short animated film *Finland's Hundred Years of Colonialism* (2017).

Music

Yoiks by Sámi artists are readily accessible on common online video portals. "Sápmi in Eurovision" is a useful overview of Eurovision Song Contest entries involving Sámi artists, from Mattis Hætta's duet with Sverre Kjelsberg in 1980 to Fred Buljo's performance with KEiiNO in 2019. Audio recordings by the band Deatnogátte Nuorat (also known under the Norwegian name Tanabreddens

Ungdom), which paved the way for Sámi pop in the 1970s, are also available.

You will find many videos with Mari Boine, among them songs from a stunning performance at the Oslo Opera House in 2009. Powerful music videos by Sofia Jannok are "This Is My Land" and "We Are Still Here." A special performance by Maxida Märak is her rendition of "My People" with Mohican musician Bill Miller.

For contemporary Sámi pop/rock acts, look for videos by SomBy, The BlackSheeps, Biru Baby, Máddji, and Ella Marie Hætta Isaksen and her band ISÁK. Kitok's "Paradise Jokkmokk" is a personal favorite. Rap enthusiasts ought to check out Duolva Duottar, SlinCraze, Áilu Valle, and Amoc.

Websites

Several Sámi websites carry general information and news articles in English. These include the websites of the Sámi Information Center (*Samiskt informationscentrum*) in Sweden (www.samer.se), of Yle Sápmi, the Sámi public broadcasting service in Finland (www.yle.fi/uutiset/osasto/sapmi), and of the Sámi Council (www.saamicouncil.net). The *Barents Observer* (www.thebarentsobserver.com), an online newspaper covering the Barents Region and the Arctic, also publishes articles on Sápmi regularly.

There is an increasing number of activist websites with pages in English. They include www.moratoriadoaimmahat.org of the activist group Ellos Deatnu!, www.350.org of the Run for Your Life project, and www.pileosapmi.com, maintained by Máret Ánne Sara. The website of the arts collective Suohpanterror (www.suohpanterror.com) contains plenty of visual material.

Both the Sámi Cultural Center of North America (www.samiculturalcenter.org) and the Pacific Sámi Searvi (www.pacificsamisearvi.org) maintain websites with valuable historical information. The website of *Baiki: The International Sámi Journal* (www.saamibaiki.org) also has very useful pages, particularly on the history of the Sámi diaspora in North America. Numerous articles about Sápmi are archived online by the Liberal Arts Instructional Technology Services (LAITS) of the University of Texas, but finding them can be a challenge. Use www.laits.utexas.edu as an entry page and search for "Sámi" and related terms.

Sámi artist Hans Ragnar Mathisen maintains a website with a wealth of material on Sámi history, culture, and politics, much of it in English (www.keviselie-hansragnarmathisen. net). Interesting entries in English can also be found on the blog of multilingual Sámi author Johan Sandberg McGuinne (www. johansandbergmcguinne.wordpress.com).

About the Author

Gabriel Kuhn is an Austrian-born author and translator living in Sweden.

More PM Press titles by Gabriel Kuhn

Life Under the Jolly Roger: Reflections on Golden Age Piracy (2010; second ed. 2020)

Sober Living for the Revolution: Hardcore Punk, Straight Edge, and Radical Politics (2010)

Soccer vs. the State: Tackling Football and Radical Politics (2011; second ed. 2019)

All Power to the Councils! A Documentary History of the German Revolution of 1918–1919 (2012)

Turning Money into Rebellion: The Unlikely Story of Denmark's Revolutionary Bank Robbers (2014)

Playing as if the World Mattered: An Illustrated History of Activism in Sports (2015)

Antifascism, Sports, Sobriety: Forging a Militant Working-Class Culture (2017)

X: Straight Edge and Radical Sobriety (2019)

ABOUT PM PRESS

PM Press is an independent, radical publisher of books and media to educate, entertain, and inspire. Founded in 2007 by a small group of people with decades of publishing, media, and organizing experience, PM Press amplifies the voices of radical authors, artists, and activists. Our aim is to deliver bold political ideas and vital stories to all walks of life and arm the dreamers to demand the impossible. We have sold millions of copies of our books, most often one at a time, face to face. We're old enough to know what we're doing and young enough to know what's at stake. Join us to create a better world.

PM Press
PO Box 23912
Oakland, CA 94623
www.pmpress.org

PM Press in Europe
europe@pmpress.org
www.pmpress.org.uk

FRIENDS OF PM PRESS

These are indisputably momentous times—the financial system is melting down globally and the Empire is stumbling. Now more than ever there is a vital need for radical ideas.

In the years since its founding—and on a mere shoestring—PM Press has risen to the formidable challenge of publishing and distributing knowledge and entertainment for the struggles ahead. With over 450 releases to date, we have published an impressive and stimulating array of literature, art, music, politics, and culture. Using every available medium, we've succeeded in connecting those hungry for ideas and information to those putting them into practice.

Friends of PM allows you to directly help impact, amplify, and revitalize the discourse and actions of radical writers, filmmakers, and artists. It provides us with a stable foundation from which we can build upon our early successes and provides a much-needed subsidy for the materials that can't necessarily pay their own way. You can help make that happen—and receive every new title automatically delivered to your door once a month—by joining as a Friend of PM Press. And, we'll throw in a free T-shirt when you sign up.

Here are your options:

- **$30 a month** Get all books and pamphlets plus 50% discount on all webstore purchases

- **$40 a month** Get all PM Press releases (including CDs and DVDs) plus 50% discount on all webstore purchases

- **$100 a month** Superstar—Everything plus PM merchandise, free downloads, and 50% discount on all webstore purchases

For those who can't afford $30 or more a month, we have **Sustainer Rates** at $15, $10 and $5. Sustainers get a free PM Press T-shirt and a 50% discount on all purchases from our website.

Your Visa or Mastercard will be billed once a month, until you tell us to stop. Or until our efforts succeed in bringing the revolution around. Or the financial meltdown of Capital makes plastic redundant. Whichever comes first.

Life Under the Jolly Roger: Reflections on Golden Age Piracy

Gabriel Kuhn

ISBN: 978-1-62963-793-8
$20.00   320 pages

Over the last couple of decades, an ideological battle has raged over the political legacy and cultural symbolism of the "golden age" pirates who roamed the seas between the Caribbean Islands and the Indian Ocean from 1690 to 1725. They are depicted as romanticized villains on the one hand and as genuine social rebels on the other. *Life Under the Jolly Roger* examines the political and cultural significance of these nomadic outlaws by relating historical accounts to a wide range of theoretical concepts—reaching from Marshall Sahlins and Pierre Clastres to Mao Zedong and Eric J. Hobsbawm via Friedrich Nietzsche and Michel Foucault. With daring theoretical speculation and passionate, respectful inquiry, Gabriel Kuhn skillfully contextualizes and analyzes the meanings of race, gender, sexuality, and disability in golden age pirate communities, while also surveying the breathtaking array of pirates' forms of organization, economy, and ethics.

Life Under the Jolly Roger also provides an extensive catalog of scholarly references for the academic reader. Yet this delightful and engaging study is written in language that is wholly accessible for a wide audience.

This expanded second edition includes an appendix with interviews about contemporary piracy, the ongoing fascination with pirate imagery, and the thorny issue of colonial implications in the romanticization of pirates.

"In addition to history Gabriel Kuhn's radical piratology brings philosophy, ethnography, and cultural studies to the stark question of the time: which were the criminals—bankers and brokers or sailors and slaves? By so doing he supplies us with another case where the history isn't dead, it's not even past!"
—Peter Linebaugh, author of *The London Hanged* and coauthor of *The Many-Headed Hydra*

"Gabriel Kuhn does a masterful job of, piece by piece, dismantling all the popular myths about golden age piracy. And then, more masterfully still, he picks up the pieces and weaves together an understanding of why, knowing what we know, we still love us some goddamn pirates."
—Margaret Killjoy, author of *The Lamb Will Slaughter the Lion* and *The Barrow Will Send What It May*

500 Years of Indigenous Resistance

Gord Hill

ISBN: 978-1-60486-106-8
$12.00   96 pages

The history of the colonization of the Americas by Europeans is often portrayed as a mutually beneficial process, in which "civilization" was brought to the Natives, who in return shared their land and cultures. A more critical history might present it as a genocide in which Indigenous peoples were helpless victims, overwhelmed and awed by European military power. In reality, neither of these views is correct.

500 Years of Indigenous Resistance is more than a history of European colonization of the Americas. In this slim volume, Gord Hill chronicles the resistance by Indigenous peoples, which limited and shaped the forms and extent of colonialism. This history encompasses North and South America, the development of nation-states, and the resurgence of Indigenous resistance in the post-WW2 era.

Gord Hill is a member of the Kwakwaka'wakw nation on the Northwest Coast. Writer, artist, and militant, he has been involved in Indigenous resistance, anti-colonial and anti-capitalist movements for many years, often using the pseudonym Zig Zag.

Wielding Words like Weapons: Selected Essays in Indigenism, 1995-2005

Ward Churchill
with a Foreword by Barbara Alice Mann

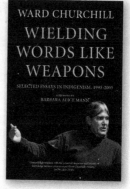

ISBN: 978-1-62963-101-1
$27.95   616 pages

Wielding Words like Weapons is a collection of acclaimed American Indian Movement activist-intellectual Ward Churchill's essays in indigenism, selected from material written during the decade 1995-2005. It includes a range of formats, from sharply framed book reviews and equally pointed polemics and op-eds to more formal essays designed to reach both scholarly and popular audiences. The selection also represents the broad range of topics addressed in Churchill's scholarship, including the fallacies of archeological and anthropological orthodoxy such as the insistence of "cannibalogists" that American Indians were traditionally maneaters, Hollywood's cinematic degradations of native people, questions of American Indian identity, the historical and ongoing genocide of North America's native peoples and the systematic distortion of the political and legal history of U.S.-Indian relations.

Less typical of Churchill's oeuvre are the essays commemorating Cherokee anthropologist Robert K. Thomas and Yankton Sioux legal scholar and theologian Vine Deloria Jr. More unusual still is his profoundly personal effort to come to grips with the life and death of his late wife, Leah Renae Kelly, thereby illuminating in very human terms the grim and lasting effects of Canada's residential schools upon the country's indigenous peoples.

A foreword by Seneca historian Barbara Alice Mann describes the sustained efforts by police and intelligence agencies as well as university administrators and other academic adversaries to discredit or otherwise "neutralize" both the man and his work. Also included are both the initial "stream-of-consciousness" version of Churchill's famous—or notorious—"little Eichmanns" opinion piece analyzing the causes of the attacks on 9/11, as well as the counterpart essay in which his argument was fully developed.

"Compellingly original, with the powerful eloquence and breadth of knowledge we have come to expect from Churchill's writing."
—Howard Zinn

"This is insurgent intellectual work—breaking new ground, forging new paths, engaging us in critical resistance."
—bell hooks